Bloom's BioCritiques

Bloom's BioCritiques

ARTHUR MILLER

Edited and with an introduction by
Harold Bloom
Sterling Professor of the Humanities
Yale University

CHELSEA HOUSE
P U B L I S H E R S
A Haights Cross Communications Company

Philadelphia

Printed and bound in the United States of America

10 9 8 7 6 5 4 3 2 1

Library of Congress Cataloging-in-Publication Data

Arthur Miller / editor, Harold Bloom ; contributing editor, Neil Heims.
    p. cm. -- (Bloom's biocritiques)
Includes biographical references and index.
  ISBN 0-7910-6188-4
  1. Miller, Arthur, 1915---Criticism and interpretation. I. Bloom,
Harold. II. Heims, Neil. III. Series.
  PS3525.I5156 Z5143 2002
  812'.52--dc21

                                                    2002008451

Chelsea House Publishers
1974 Sproul Road, Suite 400
Broomall, PA 19008-0914

http://www.chelseahouse.com

Contributing editor: Neil Heims

Cover design by Keith Trego

Cover image by Archive Photos/Getty Images

Layout by EJB Publishing Services

CONTENTS

User's Guide

These volumes are designed to introduce the reader to the life and work of the world's literary masters. Each volume begins with Harold Bloom's essay "The Work in the Writer" and a volume-specific introduction also written by Professor Bloom. Following these unique introductions is an engaging biography that discusses the major life events and important literary accomplishments of the author under consideration.

Furthermore, each volume includes an original critique that not only traces the themes, symbols, and ideas apparent in the author's works, but strives to put those works into a cultural and historical perspective. In addition to the original critique is a brief selection of significant critical essays previously published on the author and his or her works followed by a concise and informative chronology of the writer's life. Finally, each volume concludes with a bibliography of the writer's works, a list of additional readings, and an index of important themes and ideas.

HAROLD BLOOM

The Work in the Writer

Literary biography found its masterpiece in James Boswell's *Life of Samuel Johnson*. Boswell, when he treated Johnson's writings, implicitly commented upon Johnson as found in his work, even as in the great critic's life. Modern instances of literary biography, such as Richard Ellmann's lives of W. B. Yeats, James Joyce, and Oscar Wilde, essentially follow in Boswell's pattern.

That the writer somehow is in the work, we need not doubt, though with William Shakespeare, writer-of-writers, we almost always need to rely upon pure surmise. The exquisite rancidities of the Problem Plays or Dark Comedies seem to express an extraordinary estrangement of Shakespeare from himself. When we read or attend *Troilus and Cressida* and *Measure for Measure*, we may be startled by particular speeches of Ulysses in the first play, or of Vincentio in the second. These speeches, of Ulysses upon hierarchy or upon time, or of Duke Vincentio upon death, are too strong either for their contexts or for the characters of their speakers. The same phenomenon occurs with Parolles, the military impostor of *All's Well That Ends Well*. Utterly disgraced, he nevertheless affirms: "Simply the thing I am/Shall make me live."

In Shakespeare, more even than in his peers, Dante and Cervantes, meaning always starts itself again through excess or overflow. The strongest of Shakespeare's creatures—Falstaff, Hamlet, Iago, Lear, Cleopatra—have an exuberance that is fiercer than their plays can contain. If Ben Jonson was at all correct in his complaint that "Shakespeare wanted art," it could have been only in a sense that he may not have intended. Where do the personalities of Falstaff or Hamlet touch a limit? What was it in Shakespeare that made the two parts of *Henry IV* and *Hamlet* into "plays unlimited"? Neither Falstaff nor Hamlet will be stopped: their wit, their beautiful, laughing speech, their intensity of being—all these are virtually infinite.

In what ways do Falstaff and Hamlet manifest the writer in the work? Evidently, we can never know, or know enough to answer with any authority. But what would happen if we reversed the question, and asked: How did the work form the writer, Shakespeare?

Of Shakespeare's inwardness, his biography tells us nothing. And yet, to an astonishing extent, Shakespeare created our inwardness. At the least, we can speculate that Shakespeare so lived his life as to conceal the depths of his nature, particularly as he rather prematurely aged. We do not have Shakespeare on Shakespeare, as any good reader of the Sonnets comes to realize: they do not constitute a key that unlocks his heart. No sequence of sonnets could be less confessional or more powerfully detached from the poet's self.

The German poet and universal genius, Goethe, affords a superb contrast to Shakespeare. Of Goethe's life, we know more than everything; I wonder sometimes if we know as much about Napoleon or Freud or any other human being who ever has lived, as we know about Goethe. Everywhere, we can find Goethe in his work, so much so that Goethe seems to crowd the writing out, just as Byron and Oscar Wilde seem to usurp their own literary accomplishments. Goethe, cunning beyond measure, nevertheless invested a rival exuberance in his greatest works that could match his personal charisma. The sublime outrageousness of the Second Part of *Faust*, or of the greater lyric and meditative poems, form a Counter-Sublime to Goethe's own daemonic intensity.

Goethe was fascinated by the daemonic in himself; we can doubt that Shakespeare had any such interests. Evidently, Shakespeare abandoned his acting career just before he composed *Measure for Measure* and *Othello*. I surmise that the egregious interventions by Vincentio and Iago displace the actor's energies into a new kind of mischief-making, a fresh opening to a subtler playwriting-within-the-play.

But what had opened Shakespeare to this new awareness? The answer is the work in the writer, *Hamlet* in Shakespeare. One can go further: it was not so much the play, *Hamlet*, as the character Hamlet, who changed Shakespeare's art forever.

Hamlet's personality is so large and varied that it rivals Goethe's own. Ironically Goethe's Faust, his Hamlet, has no personality at all, and is as colorless as Shakespeare himself seems to have chosen to be. Yet nothing could be more colorful than the Second Part of *Faust*, which is peopled by an astonishing array of monsters, grotesque devils, and classical ghosts.

A contrast between Shakespeare and Goethe demonstrates that in each—but in very different ways—we can better find the work in the person, than we can discover that banal entity, the person in the work. Goethe to many of his contemporaries, seemed to be a mortal god. Shakespeare, so far as we know, seemed an affable, rather ordinary fellow, who aged early and became somewhat withdrawn. Yet Faust, though Mephistopheles battles for his soul, is hardly worth the trouble unless you take him as an idea and not as a person. Hamlet is nearly every-idea-in-one, but he is precisely a personality and a person.

Would Hamlet be so astonishingly persuasive if his father's ghost did not haunt him? Falstaff is more alive than Prince Hal, who says that the devil haunts him in the shape of an old fat man. Three years before composing the final *Hamlet*, Shakespeare invented Falstaff, who then never ceased to haunt his creator. Falstaff and Hamlet may be said to best represent the work in the writer, because their influence upon Shakespeare was prodigious. W.H. Auden accurately observed that Falstaff possesses infinite energy: never tired, never bored, and absolutely both witty and happy until Hal's rejection destroys him. Hamlet too has infinite energy, but in him it is more curse than blessing.

Falstaff and Hamlet can be said to occupy the roles in Shakespeare's invented world that Sancho Panza and Don Quixote possess in Cervantes's. Shakespeare's plays from 1610 on (starting with *Twelfth Night*) are thus analogous to the Second Part of Cervantes's epic novel. Sancho and the Don overtly jostle Cervantes for authorship in the Second Part, even as Cervantes battles against the impostor who has pirated a continuation of his work. As a dramatist, Shakespeare manifests the work in the writer more indirectly. Falstaff's prose genius is revived in the scapegoating of Malvolio by Maria and Sir Toby Belch, while Falstaff's darker insights are developed by Feste's melancholic wit. Hamlet's intellectual resourcefulness, already deadly, becomes poisonous in Iago and in Edmund. Yet we have not crossed into the deeper abysses of the work in the writer in later Shakespeare.

No fictive character, before or since, is Falstaff's equal in self-trust. Sir John, whose delight in himself is contagious, has total confidence both in his self-awareness and in the resources of his language. Hamlet, whose self is as strong, and whose language is as copious, nevertheless distrusts both the self and language. Later Shakespeare is, as it were, much under the influence both of Falstaff and of Hamlet, but they tug him in opposite directions. Shakespeare's own copiousness of language is well-nigh incredible: a vocabulary in excess of twenty-one thousand words, almost eighteen hundred of which he coined himself. And of his word-hoard, nearly half are used only once each, as though the perfect setting for each had been found, and need not be repeated. Love for language and faith in language are Falstaffian attributes. Hamlet will darken both that love and that faith in Shakespeare, and perhaps the Sonnets can best be read as Falstaff and Hamlet counterpointing against one another.

Can we surmise how aware Shakespeare was of Falstaff and Hamlet, once they had played themselves into existence? *Henry IV, Part I* appeared in six quarto editions during Shakespeare's lifetime; *Hamlet* possibly had four. Falstaff and Hamlet were played again and again at the Globe, but Shakespeare knew also that they were being read, and he must have had contact with some of those readers. What would it have been like to discuss Falstaff or Hamlet with one of their early readers (presumably also part of their audience at the Globe), if you were the creator of such demiurges? The question would seem nonsensical to most Shakespeare scholars, but then these days they tend to be either ideologues or moldy figs. How can we recover the uncanniness of Falstaff and of Hamlet, when they now have become so familiar?

A writer's influence upon himself is an unexplored problem in criticism, but such an influence is never free from anxieties. The biocritical problem (which this series attempts to explore) can be divided into two areas, difficult to disengage fully. Accomplished works affect the author's life, and also affect her subsequent writings. It is simpler for me to surmise the effect of *Mrs. Dalloway* and *To the Lighthouse* upon Woolf's late *Between the Acts*, than it is to relate Clarissa Dalloway's suicide and Lily Briscoe's capable endurance in art to the tragic death and complex life of Virginia Woolf.

There are writers whose lives were so vivid that they seem sometimes to obscure the literary achievement: Byron, Wilde, Malraux, Hemingway. But most major Western writers do not live that exuberantly, and the greatest of all, Shakespeare, sometimes appears to have adopted the personal mask of colorlessness. And yet there are heroes of literature who struggled titanically with their own eras—Tolstoy, Milton, Victor Hugo—who nevertheless matter more for their works than their lives.

There are great figures—Emily Dickinson, Wallace Stevens, Willa Cather—who seem to have had so little of the full intensity of life when compared to the vitality of their work, that we might almost speak of the work in the work, rather than even of the work in a person. Emily Brontë might well be the extreme instance of such a visionary, surpassing William Blake in that one regard.

I conclude this general introduction to a series of literary bio-critiques by stating a tentative formula or principle for gauging the many ways in which the work influences the person and her subsequent, later work. Our influence upon ourselves is always related to the Shakespearean invention of self-overhearing, which I have written about in several other contexts. Life, as well as poetry and prose, is overheard rather than simply heard. The writer listens to herself as though she were somebody else, and the will to change begins to operate. The forces that live in us include the prior work we have done, and the dreams and waking visions that evade our dismissals.

HAROLD BLOOM

Introduction

Rather like Eugene O'Neill before him, Arthur Miller raises, at least for me, the difficult critical question as to whether there is not an element in drama that is other than literary, even contrary in value (supposed or real) to literary values, perhaps even to aesthetic values. O'Neill, a very nearly great dramatist, particularly in *The Iceman Cometh* and *Long Day's Journey into Night*, is not a good writer, except perhaps in his stage directions. Miller is by no means a bad writer, but he is scarcely an eloquent master of the language. I have just reread *All My Sons*, *Death of a Salesman*, and *The Crucible*, and am compelled to reflect how poorly they reread, though all of them, properly staged, are very effective dramas, and *Death of a Salesman* is considerably more than that. It ranks with *Iceman*, *Long Day's Journey*, Williams's *A Streetcar Named Desire*, Wilder's *The Skin of Our Teeth* and Albee's *The Zoo Story* as one of the half-dozen crucial American plays. Yet its literary status seems to me somewhat questionable, which returns me to the issue of what there is in drama that can survive indifferent or even poor writing.

Defending *Death of a Salesman*, despite what he admits is a sentimental glibness in its prose, Kenneth Tynan memorably observed: "But the theater is an impure craft, and *Death of a Salesman* organizes its impurities with an emotional effect unrivalled in postwar drama." The observation still seems true, long after Tynan made it, yet how unlikely a similar statement would seem if ventured about Ibsen, Miller's prime precursor. Do we speak of *Hedda Gabler* organizing its impurities with an unrivalled emotional effect? Why is the American drama, except for Thornton Wilder (its one great sport), addicted to an organization of impurities, a critical phrase perhaps applicable only to Theodore Dreiser, among the major American novelists? Why is it that we have brought forth *The Scarlet Letter, Moby-Dick, Adventures of Huckleberry Finn, The Portrait of a Lady, The Sun Also Rises, The Great Gatsby, As I Lay Dying, Miss Lonelyhearts, The Crying of Lot 49*, but no comparable dramas? How can a nation whose poets include Whitman, Dickinson, Frost, Stevens, Eliot, Hart Crane, Elizabeth Bishop, James Merrill, and John Ashbery, among so many others of the highest aesthetic dignity— how can it offer us only O'Neill, Miller, and Williams as its strongest playwrights?

Drama at its most eminent tends not to appear either too early or too late in any national literature. The United States may be the great exception, since before O'Neill we had little better than Clyde Fitch, and our major dramas (it is to be hoped) have not yet manifested themselves. I have seen little speculation upon this matter, with the grand exception of Alvin B. Kernan, the magisterial scholarly critic of Shakespeare and of Elizabethan dramatic literature. Meditating upon American plays, in 1967, Kernan tuned his initially somber notes to hopeful ones:

> Thus with all our efforts, money, and good intentions, we have not yet achieved a theater; and we have not, I believe, because we do not see life in historic and dramatic terms. Even our greatest novelists and poets, sensitive and subtle though they are, do not think dramatically, and should not be asked to, for they express themselves and us in other forms more suited to their visions (and ours). But we have come very close at moments to having great plays, if not a great theatrical tradition. When the Tyrone family stands in its parlor looking at the mad mother holding her wedding dress and knowing that all the good will in the world cannot undo what the past has done to them; when Willy Loman, the salesman, plunges again and again into the past to search for the point where it all went irremediably wrong and cannot find any one fatal turning point; when the Antrobus family, to end on a more cheerful note, drafts stage hands from backstage to take the place of sick actors, gathers its feeble

and ever-disappointed hopes, puts its miserable home together again after another in a series of unending disasters stretching from the ice age to the present; then we are very close to accepting our entanglement in the historical process and our status as actors, which may in time produce a true theater.

That time has not yet come, some thirty years later, but I think that Kernan was more right even than he knew. Our greatest novelists and poets continue not to see life in historic and dramatic terms, precisely because our literary tradition remains incurably Emersonian, and Emerson shrewdly dismissed both history and drama as European rather than American. An overtly anti-Emersonian poet-novelist like Robert Penn Warren does see life in historic and dramatic terms, and yet has done his best work away from the stage, despite his effort to write *All the King's Men* as a play. Our foremost novelist, Henry James, failed as a dramatist, precisely because he was more Emersonian than he knew, and turned too far inward in nuanced vision for a play to be his proper mode of representation. One hardly sees Faulkner or Frost, Hemingway or Stevens as dramatists, though they all made their attempts. Nor would a comparison of *The Waste Land* and *The Family Reunion* be kind to Eliot's dramatic ambitions. The American literary mode, whether narrative or lyric, tends towards romance and rumination, or fantastic vision, rather than drama. Emerson, genius of the shores of America, directed us away from history, and distrusted drama as a revel. Nothing is got for nothing; Faulkner and Wallace Stevens, aesthetic light-years beyond O'Neill and Tennessee Williams, seem to mark the limits of the literary imagination in our American century. It is unfair to *All My Sons* and *Death of a Salesman* to read them with the high expectations we rightly bring to *As I Lay Dying* and *Notes Toward a Supreme Fiction*. Miller, a social dramatist, keenly aware of history, fills an authentic American need, certainly for his own time.

II

All My Sons (1947), Miller's first success, retains the flavor of post–World War II America, though it is indubitably something beyond a period piece. Perhaps all of Miller's work could be titled *The Guilt of the Fathers*, which is a dark matter for a Jewish playwright, brought up to believe in the normative tradition, with its emphasis upon the virtues of the fathers. Though it is a truism to note that *All My Sons* is an Ibsenite play, the influence relation to Ibsen remains authentic, and is part of the play's meaning, in the sense that Ibsen too is one of the fathers, and shares in their guilt. Ibsen's peculiar guilt in *All My Sons* is to have appropriated most of Miller's available stock of dramatic language. The result is that this drama is admirably constructed yet not adequately expressed. It is not just that eloquence is lacking; sometimes the characters seem unable to say what they need to say if we are to be with them as we should.

Joe Keller ought to be the hero-villain of *All My Sons*, since pragmatically he certainly is a villain. But Miller is enormously fond of Joe, and so are we; he is not a good man, and yet he lives like one, in regard to family, friends, neighbors. I do not think that Miller ever is interested in Hannah Arendt's curious notion of the banality of evil. Joe is banal, and he is not evil, though his business has led him into what must be called moral idiocy, in regard to his partner, and to any world that transcends his own immediate family. Poor Joe is just not very intelligent, and it is Miller's curious gift that he can render such a man dramatically interesting. An ordinary man who wants to have a moderately good time, who wants his family never to suffer, and who lacks any imagination beyond the immediate: what is this except an authentic American Everyman? The wretched Joe simply is someone who does not know enough, indeed who scarcely knows anything at all. Nor can he learn anything. What I find least convincing in the play is Joe's moment of breaking through to a moral awareness, and a new kind of knowledge:

> MOTHER: Why are you going? You'll sleep, why are you going?
> KELLER: I can't sleep here. I'll feel better if I go.
> MOTHER: You're so foolish. Larry was your son too, wasn't he? You know he'd never tell you to do this.
> KELLER, *looking at letter in his hand*: Then what is this if it isn't telling me? Sure, he was my son. But I think to him they were all my sons. And I guess they were, I guess they were. I'll be right down. *Exits into house.*
> MOTHER, *to Chris, with determination*: You're not going to take him!

CHRIS: I'm taking him.
MOTHER: It's up to you, if you tell him to stay he'll stay.
Go and tell him!
CHRIS: Nobody could stop him now.
MOTHER: You'll stop him! How long will he live in prison?
Are you trying to kill him?

Nothing in Joe is spiritually capable of seeing and saying: "They were all my sons. And I guess they were, I guess they were." That does not reverberate any more persuasively than Chris crying out: "There's a universe of people outside and you're responsible to it." Drama fails Miller there, or perhaps he fails drama. Joe Keller was too remote from a felt sense of reality for Miller to represent the estrangement properly, except in regard to the blindness Joe manifested towards his two sons. Miller crossed over into his one permanent achievement when he swerved from Ibsen into the marginal world of *Death of a Salesman*, where the pain is the meaning, and the meaning has a repressed but vital relationship to the normative vision that informs Jewish memory.

III

The strength of *Death of a Salesman* may be puzzling, and yet is beyond dispute; the continued vitality of the play cannot be questioned. Whether it has the aesthetic dignity of tragedy is not clear, but no other American play is worthier of the term, so far. I myself resist the drama each time I reread it, because it seems that its language will not hold me, and then I see it played on stage, and I yield to it. Miller has caught an American kind of suffering that is also a universal mode of pain, quite possibly because his hidden paradigm for his American tragedy is an ancient Jewish one. Willy Loman is hardly a biblical figure, and he is not supposed to be Jewish, yet something crucial in him is Jewish, and the play does belong to that undefined entity we can call Jewish literature, just as Pinter's *The Caretaker* rather surprisingly does. The only meaning of Willy Loman is the pain he suffers, and the pain his fate causes us to suffer. His tragedy makes sense only in the Freudian world of repression, which happens also to be the world of normative Jewish memory. It is a world in which everything has already happened, in which there never can be anything new again, because there is total sense or meaningfulness in everything, which is to say, in which everything hurts.

That cosmos informed by Jewish memory is the secret strength or permanent coherence of *Death of a Salesman*, and accounts for its ability to withstand the shrewd critique of Eric Bentley, who found that the genres of tragedy and of social drama destroyed one another here. Miller's passionate insistence upon tragedy is partly justified by Willy's perpetual sense of being in exile. Commenting on his play, Miller wrote that: "The truly valueless man, a man without ideals, is always perfectly at home anywhere." But Willy, in his own small but valid way, has his own version of the Nietzschean "desire to be elsewhere, the desire to be different," and it does reduce to a Jewish version. Doubtless, as Mary McCarthy first noted, Willy "could not be Jewish because he had to be American." Nearly forty years later, that distinction is pragmatically blurred, and we can wonder if the play might be stronger if Willy were more overtly Jewish.

We first hear Willy say: "It's all right. I came back." His last utterance is the mere repetition of the desperately hushing syllable: "Shhh!" just before he rushes out to destroy himself. A survivor who no longer desires to survive is something other than a tragic figure. Willy, hardly a figure of capable imagination, nevertheless is a representation of terrible pathos. Can we define precisely what that pathos is?

Probably the most famous speech in *Death of a Salesman* is Linda's pre-elegy for her husband, of whom she is soon to remark: "A small man can be just as exhausted as a great man." The plangency of Linda's lament has a universal poignance, even if we wince at its naked design upon us:

> Willy Loman never made a lot of money. His name was never in the paper. He's not the finest character that ever lived. But he's a human being, and a terrible thing is happening to him. So attention must be paid. He's not to be allowed to fall into his grave like an old dog. Attention, attention must be finally paid to such a person.

Behind this is Miller's belated insistence "that everyone knew Willy Loman," which is a flawed emphasis on Miller's part, since he first thought of calling the play *The Inside of His Head*, and Willy already lives in a phantasmagoria when the drama opens. You cannot know a man half lost in the American dream, a man who is unable to tell past from present. Perhaps the play should have been called *The Dying of a*

Salesman, because Willy is dying throughout. That is the pathos of Linda's passionate injunction that attention must be finally paid to such a person, a human being to whom a terrible thing is happening. Nothing finds Willy anymore; everything loses him. He is a man upon whom the sun has gone down, to appropriate a great phrase from Ezra Pound. But have we defined as yet what is particular about his pathos?

I think not. Miller, a passionate moralist, all but rabbinical in his ethical vision, insists upon giving us Willy's, and his sons', sexual infidelities as synecdoches of the failure of Willy's vision of reality. Presumably, Willy's sense of failure, his belief that he has no right to his wife, despite Linda's love for him, is what motivates Willy's deceptions, and those of his sons after him. Yet Willy is not destroyed by his sense of failure. Miller may be a better interpreter of Miller than he is a dramatist. I find it wholly persuasive that Willy is destroyed by love, by his sudden awareness that his son Biff truly loves him. Miller beautifully comments that Willy resolves to die when "he is given his existence ... his fatherhood, for which he has always striven and which until now he could not achieve." That evidently is the precise and terrible pathos of Willy's character and of his fate. He is a good man, who wants only to earn and to deserve the love of his wife and of his sons. He is self-slain, not by the salesman's dream of America, but by the universal desire to be loved by one's own, and to be loved beyond what one believes one deserves. Miller is not one of the masters of metaphor, but in *Death of a Salesman* he memorably achieves a pathos that none of us would be wise to dismiss.

COOKIE LOMMEL

Biography of Arthur Miller

LIFE OF A SALESMAN

Over six feet tall and energetic, even in his eighties, American playwright Arthur Miller stood on a street corner in New York City, surrounded by what he teasingly called his "gang." His figure was imposing—so much so that one admirer has likened his visage to those carved on Mount Rushmore. Despite Miller's comfortable attire and his willingness to joke around, bystanders remained in awe of this living legend.

As 1999 marked the 50th anniversary of *Death of Salesman*, Miller arrived at the Eugene O'Neill Theatre to see the new production of his American tragedy. Yet instead of relishing the moment, Miller expressed frustration over the fanfare and his expected participation in the opening of a play he had written 50 years before. While he seemed grateful that a car was coming to collect him from the mob in front of the theater, he was dismayed that the producers expected him to take the stage in recognition of his creation. But Miller, who Dustin Hoffman once said looks like a California redwood tree and talks like a New York taxi driver was determined to endure: "I have strong teeth, and I'll grit it out. At the same time, I'd just as soon stay home.... I suppose they'll do it, and I suppose they'll get me up, and I suppose I'll put up with it.... And I suppose I'll enjoy it."

Salesman, having enjoyed countless runs worldwide, has showcased the talents of Lee J. Cobb, George C. Scott, and Dustin Hoffman. Its main character, Willy Loman, has helped define the American identity. Yet this great drama is not the only one for which Arthur Miller is famous. Miller began his spectacular career as a playwright with the success of *All My Sons* in 1944. He also wrote such landmark dramas as *The Crucible* (based on the Salem witchcraft trials), *After the Fall*, and *A View from the Bridge*. His other works include *Incident at Vichy*, *The Price*, *The Archbishop's Ceiling*, *The American Clock*, and *A Memory of Two Mondays*. He has tried his hand at screenplays, too, and has received awards for television dramas (*Playing for Time*) and movies (*The Misfits*).

The anniversary tribute to *Salesman* featured new music and a huskier Willy Loman, played by Brian Dennehy, and yet Miller was characteristically nonchalant. Always hard on himself, and always expecting more work to be done, Miller thought that the new production of *Salesman* needed a little more work in the first act. To him, the play is always a process, and that process requires change. As he once said of *Salesman*, "Thank God, there is more than one viable way to do this play."

Often called a living treasure, Miller might be expected to be content with his accomplishments; but he continues to explore new opportunities, pursue new causes, and perhaps most importantly, to write—working not by necessity, but by choice. In his eighties, Miller still views change as a way of staying fresh and alive. Not only does he consider change as essential to being contemporary, but he views it as the "inevitable and rightful condition of all life." The plays he has written, even in his ninth decade of life, continue to receive international acclaim, while his penchant for cultural commentary remains strong, with recently published essays such as "On Politics and the Art of Acting."

RISING DRAMATIST

Arthur Asher Miller was born on October 17, 1915, to Isidore and Augusta (née Barnett) Miller. The family lived in a sixth-floor apartment in Harlem, which Miller recalls as having a wonderful view. In his youth, Miller would lay quietly on the floor of their apartment as his mother called upon the spirits to move the planchette of her Ouija board. His mother maintained connections to both the spirit world and the world of their large extended family, and Arthur noticed early that there was performance in what she was doing. Once, sitting bolt upright from a deep sleep in an Atlantic City hotel room, she had declared that her absent mother had died; she had claimed since to have sensed the loss before, or at the very time of, its occurrence. Her performances, suggesting that a world existed beyond the plane of ordinary life in 1920s New York, hardly made Miller happy, and at times left him full of fear.

Between Augusta Miller's devotion to the spirit world and his two siblings, Miller found competition for attention to be fierce. Arthur's younger sister, Joan, had usurped his title of Chief Baby, while his handsome older brother, Kermit, seemed to have inherited their father's enviable blond hair and blue eyes. Furthermore, Kermit behaved better in school than his brother did, and Augusta was ashamed to be informed so by Arthur's teacher—making Arthur feel like a disappointment to his mother. Arthur resembled his mother, small and dark in a big Polish family that found something wrong in looking small and dark. His ears protruded, and his uncle was merciless on the subject, with barbs such as "Pin back your ears, Arthur. There's a tunnel coming."

Isidore Miller, Arthur's father, was a well-off manufacturer of women's coats. His coat factory, Miltex Coat and Suit Company, provided jobs for many family members, and his wealth prompted his arranged marriage to Augusta. Life for the Millers in Harlem was comfortable. They had a chauffeur to take Isidore to work, pianos for Augusta to play, and many books. Feeling intellectually stifled, despite her books, Augusta hired a Columbia student to discuss literature with her.

After the stock market crash of 1929, the Millers' wealth quickly diminished. The family was forced to move from the Harlem apartment, where Arthur had spent the 14 years since his birth. Their new residence was in the Midwood section of Brooklyn. Unlike Harlem, a city patrolled by policemen on big horses with billy clubs, where groups of boys played "kick the can" in the streets, Midwood was still fairly rural. There were lots of elm trees, the roads were mostly unpaved, and nobody, Arthur learned to his surprise, stole his pens, galoshes, blotters, notebooks, or other school supplies if he left his seat to go to the blackboard.

His mother had relatives in this part of Brooklyn. Her father, Louis Barnett, a clothing contractor who had come from the same village in Poland as Arthur's other grandfather, also settled into the new apartment and shared a room with Arthur. Jewish people like the Barnetts and the Millers had been persecuted in Poland, and many had immigrated to the United States in search of opportunity. Arthur's forefathers viewed it as little less than a crime to pass up opportunity, and they often looked out for themselves—they were survivors in a hard world.

The grandfather who shared Arthur's room was of this very tough breed. Unlike his imaginative and well-read daughter, he seldom talked to young Arthur. Louis Barnett valued order, and he had a temper. When he disapproved of Arthur's marrying outside the Jewish community many years later, he threw a clock at Arthur's mother. He also had a strong dislike of union organizers, and is said to have lured them up to the top of the stairwell at work only to knock their heads together. As his grandfather was static and old-fashioned, Arthur did not look to him for affection.

His own father, too, had known hardship. As a seven-year-old, Isidore Miller, told that his family lacked the resources to take him to the United States, had been left behind in Poland at the time of his family's emigration. He had been passed among various relatives for months until his money arrived; then, sent to America alone, a tag around his neck, he had to ask strangers to help him onto the ship sailing for New York. His parents had been too busy to fetch him when at last he arrived and instead had sent his brother Abe, who played tricks on Isidore all the way home.

Years later, Miller transformed parts of his father's story into effective drama. When he was a young man, Isidore Miller was supposed to go on a selling trip with a suitcase full of coat samples; he went to the train station but, seized with homesickness, returned to his mother. When many years later Arthur Miller sat down in the hut he had built himself to write *Death of a Salesman*, he said that "the whole disaster in a nutshell" was a salesman who couldn't get past Yonkers. It was "the end of the world," he said. "It's like an actor saying *It's all right, I can't speak.*" Miller, talking about this play to Dan Rather in 1999, a century after Isidore's failure to board the train, said that the play was all about "conflicts between fathers and sons, sons and fathers, between the wife, the mother, and the children."

Miller was drawing on his own life. The Great Depression had had a serious effect on him as a young person—he had gone from riding in chauffeur-driven limousines to keeping a vegetable garden and fishing near Coney Island. Americans in the 1930's were ravaged by hunger and unemploy-ment. The failure of the economy of the Roaring Twenties shook Miller's faith in the capitalist economic system of his time. His plays of the 1940s, *All My Sons* and *Death of a Salesman*, reflected this disillusionment with the American dream, which had resulted from the collapse of his father's business and such a radical change of lifestyle.

This disillusionment also created conflict, which led to his distancing himself from his family. Arthur was developing ideas that were too radical to meet with his conservative immigrant grandparents' approval. He was drawn to the great Russian writers like Fyodor Dostoevsky, whose plots revolved around the suffering of characters who have been wronged by society and who in turn break society's laws.

Arthur's grades were not as high as his later talents would suggest, and he had too little money for college; thus he began work in an auto parts warehouse. He took a job as a shipping clerk, earning $15 every week.

By 1934, he moved to another state, a long way away from his family. He was granted conditional admission to the University of Michigan, where he enrolled in journalism and became an editor on the evening paper. He also developed a profound interest in the Spanish Civil War as part of the social conscience of his childhood. International volunteers were helping the Loyalists, backed by the socialist Soviet Union, to fight fascist forces backed by Adolph Hitler and Francisco Franco. The fascists won, after a million people had perished in the conflict.

Miller had considered fighting the fascists, and like many young men and women of his era, his experience during the Great Depression drew him to the ideas associated with socialism. At the same time, he was developing a passionate interest in writing. Despite his early interest in the theater—he had attended the Schubert Theater for the first time at the age of eight and had gone often ever since—Miller's first writings were not dramas. His father had loved the comedy of vaudeville and familiarized young Arthur with the conventions of the stage. As a boy, Miller had willingly entered the world of the imagination, often reading the newspaper serials in search of adventure. He had believed strongly in and breathlessly followed the story of *The Curse of King Tut's Tomb*, and he had had visions of fighting the Germans, as his uncles had done in World War I—going so far as to play in his uncle Moe's spike-topped souvenir German helmet despite his lingering fear and horror at its origin.

While attending the University of Michigan, Miller entered a drama-writing contest for the annual Avery Hopwood literary prize. He won the first-place prize of $250, and it had taken him only six days to write his winning entry, *No Villain*. The story of a New York Jewish family in the garment business, *No Villain* began the strong autobiographical streak in Miller's work. Abe Simon, the central character, is a businessman of conservative interests at odds with his wife, two sons, and daughter. Uncoincidentally, the second son attends the University of Michigan; however, the core conflict was imagined as tensions erupt when the student son returns to New York for the summer holidays and is persuaded to return to the clothing business, where his political beliefs force him to support the striking workers rather than his father. Miller's own family life was clearly transformed into a dramatic vehicle of a structure tight enough to win a prestigious student award. He would revisit these themes often in later work.

Pleased by his success, Miller switched from journalism to English and began reading the works of other dramatists, such as Henrik Ibsen, who were considered to have a modern vision. Inspired to rewrite and revise, Miller transformed *No Villian* into *They Too Arise* and won $1250 in prize money from the Bureau of New Plays. His next play, *Honors at Dawn*, brought him a second Hopwood prize. He followed *Honors* with *The Great Disobedience*, and by this time he was hooked on drama.

In 1938, Miller was graduated as a member of the Federal Theatre Project, a social program designed to help out-of-work actors, writers, and artists, but it was here that he first experienced the political persecution that culminated in 1953's *The Crucible*. The Federal Theatre Project was closed down just before the production of his *Listen My Children*, for the government believed it to be contaminated by Communist influences.

Miller, suddenly out of work, took a position in the Brooklyn Navy Yard. It was at this time that he met his first wife, Mary Grace Slattery, and married her with some difficulty—she was Catholic and he Jewish— in 1940. Neither the bride's nor the groom's family supported the match.

Miller recalled with anger that the priest clearly resented their "mixed" union and announced that "these marriages never last." Obstacles arose to receiving the special religious dispensation required for two people of different faiths to marry, humiliating and angering Miller and his new Midwestern in-laws. Finally, he and Mary were married in Ohio without his family present—they did not seem to want to come, he later said, and in any case he could not have paid their way.

After the couple had been married only a week, Miller left on a tour of the gulf ports to conduct research for a play about secret Nazi bases in the South Pacific. The subject reflected contemporary interest, as the United States was about to enter World War II. The newlyweds settled in Brooklyn, where Mary found a job as a secretary in a publishing house, and Miller wrote for radio. CBS's Columbia Workshop, for example, bought his political satire *The Pussycat and the Expert Plumber Who Was a Man*. It was broadcast while he was at sea studying gulf ports. During this time, he wrote four or five dramas, including *The Man Who Had All the Luck*, which echoed the later *Death of a Salesman*. *Luck* was the story of a Midwestern businessman certain that everyone wanted to cheat him out of his wealth. The play opened on November 23, 1944, and ran for only four performances owing to bad reviews; at the least, it taught Miller a great deal about mounting a production.

With this experience, he decided to try his hand at other forms of literature. He wrote a documentary in book form, called *Situation Normal*, about the experiences of American servicemen. He had never served in the military because of his bad knees, but his sharp eye for detail was praised in reviews of the book.

For the most part, the years of his young adulthood were spent honing his craft and developing the themes that would later recur in his most powerful works. Miller worried about the balance of self-interest with public good and agonized over the high cost of idealism. He passionately condemned prosperity based on immorality or amorality, while offering little hope that virtue would lead to success. He promoted the universal need for loving and responsible relationships. In these years, his sense of being left out from his family joined itself tightly to his vision of drama as a means of creating new life.

His new rules for drama developed from his childhood observations; "my homeland, the floor" was the source of his characters.

They came, he said, from sidewalks, not skyscrapers. His language threw off the rules for writing that had been drummed into him in childhood. He has said that when he was in grade school "[w]riting in more or less the language one spoke was a sign of poor education and vulgarity." Style was expected to be "proper" in order to uplift. He dispensed with all of that. He learned from his failed plays to place believable words, not political or social ideals, in the mouths of his characters so that the audience could identify with them.

Even in the lean years, as he struggled to be a playwright, Miller knew instinctively that what mattered most of all was that he was doing something he loved. His works have all been called "love stories" because of their ultimate insistence that the audience care deeply about the human perspective placed before them. Miller writes because it makes him happy, not for the money or the fame. "I really have no alternative," he said. "It's an act of affection and love that keeps wanting to happen again and again and again. It's a love for shaping one's feelings about life at any one moment."

THE CURTAIN GOES UP

As Miller was still trying to find his own distinct voice as a writer, a new voice was added to the family. On September 7, 1944, Mary gave birth to their only daughter and first-born child, Jane. It was a year of new beginnings, some disappointing.

Miller was working hard. While most of his money came from radio dramas for NBC and CBS, a real theater production, one on the Great White Way of Broadway, however, eluded the playwright. For three years he searched for a production of *The Man Who Had All the Luck*. The same year of Jane's birth, Miller's play had its Broadway debut but closed after four performances. It was his first failure, but inside this heartbreaking experience were the seeds of a great play, a masterpiece.

Miller told himself that he would never write another play. After endless drafts and rewrites of *Luck*, the playwright learned a lesson. He was able to "find himself as a playwright and perhaps as a person," as he would later write in his autobiography, *Timebends*.

The Man Who Had All the Luck began as a novel, *Focus*. Published in 1945 and the only novel the author completed, *Focus* was not well received; however, the themes that would become a thread through all of Miller's work were shaped here. The story deals with anti-Jewish prejudice, a painful reality that the Second World War and Hitler's Nazi Germany had made terrifyingly real. In a coincidence of timing and luck, Miller's work led him in the direction of another play, one that would place Miller firmly onto the theater landscape.

A famous drama critic, John Anderson, met with Miller and told him that he should reconsider the original play version of *The Man Who Had All the Luck*. Miller had never met a theater critic before, but he listened to Anderson. "A doom hangs over the play," he told Miller. "Something that promises tragedy." This encounter was a turning point for Miller, and a tragedy did happen—offstage. Three weeks after their meeting, Anderson died of meningitis. Two years after that encounter, Miller finally had in his hands a labor of love, sweat, and devotion. He was 30 years old when he began *All My Sons*. Every line of the play was rewritten until perfect. Miller was driven to create something on his own terms, to give it his very best. At last, a work that was fully his own. Even if this play failed, he would have the satisfaction of having poured his entire being into it. A comment from a critic set in motion events that would mark Miller's life as a writer forever.

In his attempt to get the play produced, Miller sent *All My Sons* to Herman Shumlin, who had produced and directed the work of Lillian Hellman, one of the few American female playwrights at the time. Shumlin never read the play, so Miller sent it to his agent, Leland Hayward. When, later, Hayward admitted that he hadn't looked at it, Miller in a fit of anger demanded it be returned, along with all his other works. A secretary working for the agency intervened and, wanting to defuse the situation, asked Miller to leave the manuscript of *All My Sons* with another agent, Kay Brown.

The next day Brown sent a message to Miller. The play was terrific, she told him. What began as a frustrating attempt to have the play read, was the start of a 40-year relationship between agent and client. It was also the beginning of a director–playwright union that would produce some of the best-staged work in American theater. Miller was about to enter the world of Elia Kazan.

Peers and foes both regarded Kazan as unique and gifted. He and producer Harold Clurman worked in New York's legendary Group Theatre, a laboratory for new American plays and actors. When *All My*

Sons was presented to Kazan and Clurman, they both saw the possibilities of an important production. They weren't alone in their admiration; the Theatre Guild, another famous company at the time that had produced the work of renowned playwright Eugene O'Neill, also was considering the play. Whereas no one had been interested before, Miller now had two world-class companies vying for the chance to stage his plays.

Miller chose the Group Theatre, with Kazan as director. Kazan, who would later direct modern classics by playwright Tennessee Williams such as *A Streetcar Named Desire*, with scene-stealer Marlon Brando, had a reputation for being hard on artists, for wanting only the best. It was a good fit.

Kazan pushed and prodded Miller to rework the play. Known for wanting only what was "essential" in a work and frowning on what he called "adornments," things that didn't help the story, Kazan had an eye for truth and fine detail that suited the playwright's ideas. Kazan told Miller to write from his core. Miller revised the play, and what remained was a powerful work of art.

All My Sons premiered in 1947 in New Haven, Connecticut. When it reached the stage of the Coronet Theater in New York, Miller said it was "like a bullet on a straight clean trajectory that rammed the audience back into its seats." The play made Miller famous. Even though some critics didn't care for the work, Brooks Atkinson, a popular critic, defended Miller publicly, and critics began to take the playwright seriously. The production played for several months, and then, on May 31, his son Robert was born.

Miller was ambivalent about his fame; his newfound success made him uncomfortable. How could he stay connected with his roots, with his past, in this new world of prestige, awards, and ovations? It frightened him, and he would be in conflict with these feelings for most of his life. Why he did what came next is unclear—presumably, it was a manifestation of some guilt over his success, or an effort to reconnect— but soon after this Miller went to the New York State employment service office in search of a job as a laborer. The increasingly famous playwright took a position in Long Island City in Queens and worked on an assembly line. He earned the minimum wage putting together box dividers for beer cases. He quickly came to the conclusion that factory work was not what he was meant to do with his life and quit the job, but he was never able to ease his conscience completely. How could he write about the "common man" without *being* such a man? The problem had to be resolved gradually; Miller needed to find a way to adjust to his new life.

He moved his family to a cottage home in Roxbury, Connecticut, a haven for many writers. Money was no longer a concern, as royalties were sent weekly. This feeling of economic freedom was strangely disturbing to Miller, and he worried that he was losing touch with "ordinary lives." Ordinary people didn't write plays and have money sent. At the bottom of this anxiety, however, were deeper questions: Would this success spoil him? Would he lose touch with his artistic self? The problems were difficult, and Miller isolated himself and became withdrawn. As part of this isolation, Miller often took long, meditative walks across the Brooklyn Bridge and through his former neighborhood, where he was at home. These strolls across the Bridge seemed to him part of a common experience of the artist—that need for time to reflect, and he realized that he might have become too attached to his work. He also discovered that the very idea of creating something so private, by taking a part of his inner self and making it public, had somehow become shameful to him. His most personal thoughts were revealed to all on stage, as the artist exposed his secrets and left himself naked. Still, many more secrets of Miller's personal life would be revealed through his plays, blurring the boundaries between art and life, and out of this quiet period came a new tale to be told.

One day during such a walk, Miller noticed a bit of graffiti painted on a wall, *Dové Pete Panto?* ("Where is Pete Panto?") The question was scrawled everywhere, it seemed. He discovered that there was a connection between the scribble and a story that involved the Mafia, unions, and the mysterious disappearance of a longshoreman. By talking to men on the piers, he entered into a secret society far removed from his own world.

Miller began a screenplay about this event, and *A View from the Bridge* took the shape of a play, only to be discarded. Almost without realizing it, he was being pulled into another story—one he hadn't expected to find in the notes and abandoned manuscript, the story of a salesman.

Miller was struck with a new idea. He wanted to tell a story that felt "unreal" and "real" at the same time, a play in which the past and the present moved back and forth. He heard the single note of a flute that would be the signal for transitions between the here-and-now and the before-and-then. It was a stroke of creative brilliance. To move back and forth through time in a dreamlike state with the brightness or color of light changing the character was a truly inventive way to tell a story onstage.

His imagination opened. He had the form, or a structure, just the seeds of something—but what? The momentum was powerful, a rush. When he returned to his country home, he wanted to write the story in a single setting, but then another thought captured him. He needed a studio in which to write this new play—one that he created and built himself, with his own hands.

Miller wasn't known to be a good carpenter, but he was determined and competent. He set about the task. The physical part of creativity took over him, and he completed the studio, a space in which to produce his next work.

Miller wrote the entire first half of his new play, *Death of a Salesman*, in 24 straight hours, never taking a break, never sleeping. He had only one line to begin with. He heard a woman say, "Willy!" and a man respond, "It's all right, I came back." He thought he would never get beyond those opening lines. Another six weeks of work followed the marathon writing session before the play was finished.

The play's original title was *Death of a Salesman: Certain Private Conversations in Two Acts and a Requiem*. Miller wanted to "open" up the mind of his character, to have the audience actually see what he was thinking. In fact, he wanted to call it "The Inside of His Head." This was a dramatic departure from the way in which most plays were written.

Miller, however, thought that it was a useful device for *Death of a Salesman*. "The play's eye was to revolve from within Willy's head," Miller wrote, "sweeping endlessly in all directions like a light on the sea, and nothing that formed in the distant mist was to be left uninvestigated." As to the uniqueness of what he was creating: "[T]he artist blindly follows his nose with his hands outstretched."

The blind faith he had in his story of a little salesman turned into a play with the vitality and power and endurance that only a special breed of art can claim. With excitement and anticipation he sent the play to friend and collaborator Elia Kazan. Soon they made plans for a production.

The role of the salesman, Willy Loman, would be crucial. Willy Loman was written as a "shrimp of a man," and Miller thought it entirely wrong that Kazan wanted to have heavyset actor Lee J. Cobb play the role; but Cobb proved him wrong. The booming actor made the role his own, making it a hallmark in the theater. From the first performance at the Locust Street Theater in Philadelphia, Cobb made the character of Willy Loman a part of American history. At the final curtain, the audience didn't applaud; everyone was crying. When the play premiered at New York's Morosco Theater on February 10, 1949, one critic summarized the reaction: *Death of a Salesman* was a "time bomb."

Miller remembers much later, in *Salesman in Beijing*, that a play with the word "death" in the title alarmed 1949 producer Kermit Bloomgarden, who polled theatergoers and asked whether they would see a play called *Death of a Salesman*. Nobody said that they would. "They had a list of about fifteen titles," Miller told *The New Yorker* in 1999. "One of them was 'Free and Clear.'" It sounded ludicrous, but he never forgot it. Salesman stuck, though, and in 1949, when Miller was 35 years old, the play was awarded the Pulitzer Prize for Drama.

COMMUNISTS AND WITCHES

The early 1950s was no "simpler time"; it was a period of troubling attitudes. The war was over, television was the new national craze, and the world wondered whether humans would ever walk on the moon, or whether computers were just a passing phase. America at this time was battling its second major "red scare": McCarthyism. The tense international political situation that followed the end of World War II and the beginning of the Cold War had engendered some perceptions at the time that Communists were going to take control of the country and destroy its capitalism and democracy. Those affiliated with the Communist Party and "Communist sympathizers" were anathema, traitors to the American way of life; anyone close to the Communists, or who claimed to be one of them, was marked as un-American. Many citizens, especially those working in the entertainment industry, would fall victim to a crushing paranoia-based ostracism that would later be called the "blacklist."

The House Un-American Activities Committee (HUAC) was established to root out the leftists, and at its head was Joseph McCarthy, a U.S. senator from Wisconsin. Congressional hearings began, and people's lives were scrutinized for evidence of Communist leanings.

Reputations were ruined. Sports figures, actors, directors, writers, businesspeople, government officials—hundreds of American citizens, in every profession, were subjected to grueling investigations. Before the end of the decade, hundreds of people would be forced to answer personal questions about their lives, suffering public humiliation. The careers of many prominent people were destroyed almost instantly, often through rumor and gossip.

When Bobby Lewis, a veteran of the Group Theatre, asked Miller to adapt Henrik Ibsen's 1881 play *An Enemy of the People*, everyone familiar with the play knew that it had strong, even dangerous parallels to the times. After reading through Ibsen's work, Miller began to write, thinking that he was about to embark on a fight that Ibsen himself would have enjoyed. "As always, I would find out what I really believed through my attempts to dramatize my sense of life," Miller wrote of the period.

However, the more Miller dug in, the more he squirmed at some of the play's implications. The main character suggests that there exists a class of people who should dictate what other people should believe. To Miller, a democrat and an ardent champion of human rights, this was "a rather a large pill." But he cut through the problem by using Ibsen's ideas to address what was happening in the United States at the time. Human beings, he contended, have the right to resist any pressure to conform.

The piece premiered in 1950; it was strong but never made an impression on Broadway. Critics detected anti-American propaganda in Miller's adaptation, and its failure "opened wide the door to my time of confusion," Miller later said. The playwright withdrew into his work for some time, though perhaps not as long as he would have liked: "I should have exulted in my aloneness," he wrote, "and taken heart from Ibsen's signature line—'He is strongest who is most alone.' But the Jew in me shied from private salvation as something close to sin."

Even though Miller hated the Hollywood system—"the very process itself of exchanging art for money was repulsive"—by 1950 he was there to negotiate a film version of his longshoreman story. He would work "spec," or "on speculation," with Harry Cohn at Columbia Pictures: no money would be paid up front, and the writers and directors would be paid when the film turned a profit.

But the entertainment capital of the world was perhaps most subject to the power of McCarthyism. The question "Are you now, or have you ever been, a member of the Communist Party?" echoed in the hallways, at parties, in offices. An affirmative answer was a social and professional kiss of death, and refusal to answer, or to name friends who might also bear suspicion, risked charges of contempt of Congress—and possible imprisonment. It was a time of paranoia, and Miller was swept into the frenzy.

The Hollywood movie machine knew that working with alleged or suspected Communists was risky, for bad publicity translated into bad box office sales. Therefore, when the studio approached Miller—widely considered at least a liberal, if not outright "red"—about his possibly anti-democratic longshoreman story, it requested a few changes. It was at last agreed that Elia Kazan, who was already in Hollywood, would direct the revised film.

The collaboration with Kazan would have an effect on spheres of Miller's life other than the artistic and the professional; it was Kazan who introduced Miller to the up-and-coming starlet, a bit player in a few movies, whom Miller would later remember as "a whirling light ... all paradox and mystery, street tough one moment, then lifted by a lyrical and poetic sensitivity that few retain past early adolescence." She possessed an undeniable quality, a spark, an innocence and vulnerability packaged in an irresistible feminine appeal that was impossible to ignore. "Even after those few hours ... she had taken on an immanence in my imagination, the vitality of a force one does not understand," Miller later recalled. The woman was Marilyn Monroe, and a part of Miller wanted to be *her* salvation.

Meanwhile, Cohn had submitted Miller's screenplay to the Federal Bureau of Investigation (FBI) for scrutiny. The FBI told Kazan that the premise, of corruption on the piers and in the unions in Brooklyn, was untrue and therefore shouldn't be made into a film. It suggested that Miller rewrite the story, making the "bad guys" into members of the Communist Party. Miller refused, and production was stopped.

The "red scare" affected Miller profoundly. He searched for a symbol, a metaphor, to describe what was happening, and his memory offered the story of the seventeenth-century witch trials in Salem, Massachusetts. Coincidence soon led him to a book on the very topic: Marion Starkey's *The Devil in Massachusetts*, a history of the persecution and trials of the accused. Miller was eager to learn more.

A trip to Salem in 1952 was the first step in a long journey to create his next drama. Looking through the public records of the trials, Miller saw easy parallels between the fear and corruption of that time and the events he and his peers were currently living through. A theme was emerging: what happens when humans "project their own feelings of vileness onto others"? It was a human thing to do, and the consequences could be devastating. In Salem, women were burned to death. Miller was again at work in the realm of tragedy, and the work quickly took off. When *The Crucible* was ready, he sent it to director Jed Harris, and together they polished it for its premiere.

Unfortunately, working with Harris became a disaster. Miller didn't like Harris's interpretation or his direction and called Harris's vision of the play "an invitation to slumber" that played "stiff" and "formal," without any energy. During rehearsals Harris became ill, leaving the production in the hands of the playwright himself. When Harris returned, he was fired and Miller worked with the actors officially, but Miller was never sure of himself; although *The Crucible* did well in its first public performance in Wilmington, Delaware, the playwright thought that the production was "dead on stage" and that Harris's tactics had killed it. When *The Crucible* finally opened at the Martin Beck Theater in January 1953, the New York production confirmed his feelings.

This was the year of some of the HUAC's most intense investigations and trials. *The Crucible* seemed a thinly disguised reenactment, and the audience wasn't polite in recognizing the fact. The reviews were mixed, but the audience responded negatively, even with open hostility. After two months, the play closed.

Some critics believed the play struck too close to what was happening at the time; nevertheless, the play received several important awards, and *The Crucible* has become one of Miller's most frequently produced works. "One of the strongest urges in the writer's heart," Miller has written, "and perhaps most especially the American's, is to reveal what has been hidden and denied, and rend the veil." The playwright as moralist became the creator of plays with a social conscience; but if art imitated life, then Miller's life would now become an imitation of his art.

In 1955 Miller's passport was revoked after he returned from a production of *The Crucible* in Brussels, Belgium. Another blow came later in that year, when he was commissioned by a young producer for a project funded by the City of New York to write a screenplay about juvenile delinquency and gang warfare. HUAC investigator Dolores Scotti paid a visit to the officials in charge of the production, and warned them that associating with Miller's "communism" might prove embarrassing to them. The producer was fired, and the officials had to vote whether they could still work with Miller on the screenplay. When Miller refused to divulge his beliefs or answer personal questions, they voted him off the project. He lost by one vote.

He was losing confidence as a playwright as well. At the request of his friend and fellow thespian Martin Ritt, Miller worked furiously and completed his one-act play, *A Memory of Two Mondays*, in less than two weeks. Ritt and the acting troupe set to perform it loved the piece, but Ritt wanted another play to round off the evening—in his own words, a "curtain raiser." Miller completed his one-act play *An Italian Tragedy*, today known as *A View from the Bridge*, in just over a week. These plays were never produced with Ritt's of actors.

Still looking to see his works performed, Miller called his old friend, the producer Kermit Bloomgarden, and the two agreed to prepare the plays for the stage. After the New York debut, Miller re-wrote *A View from the Bridge*, the longshoreman piece, into a full-length play for a production in London, under Peter Brook. It was a frustrating premiere: this story of an Italian longshoreman and his struggle to keep his family together did better in London than it was doing in New York, Miller's hometown. The work was not fulfilling him.

Also, there were problems at home that he could not ignore. The focus of his affections was shifting and splitting, and his life was "colliding with itself." His wife and girlfriend and the government hovered over him, forming a complex web from which he could not escape.

THE LONG-AWAITED MARRIAGE

Marilyn Monroe had awed Miller at their first meeting, but he hadn't pursued her. Indeed, the courtship had been reversed: Monroe had written notes to *him*, in a slanted scrawl, in various pens and pencils, asking when they could see each other again. Miller had written back, explaining to the woman whom every man in America yearned for that he was not the man for her—that he couldn't be. In his journals, though, he had spoken the truth: she had charmed him already.

By the time Miller came into Monroe's life, her Hollywood fame was taking its toll. She had built a career on "dumb-blondness" but now wanted to be respected as a serious actress. She had earned a reputation as difficult to work with; she was late to film sets, abused sleeping pills and alcohol, couldn't remember her lines, and was fired from several acting jobs. "Hollywood is a place where they'll pay you a thousand dollars for a kiss and fifty cents for your soul," Monroe once said about the studio system. Her professional insecurities were in full bloom.

The two became seriously involved, and what had begun as a flirtation was consuming Miller. He was afraid of his attachment, but equally afraid of living without Monroe. His marriage, once a sanctuary, was failing, admittedly or not. The traveling, the long trips away, the conflict of his art and the hysteria of the witch-hunts, all combined to at once exhilarate and confuse him; but, as conflicted as he was, in 1956 he formally divorced Mary Slattery. He traveled to Nevada for a quick divorce, but the state required six weeks of residency before a divorce could be filed and finalized, so he complied. The tranquility and the sheer beauty of his surroundings helped him to sort out his feelings after what he would later refer to as "exploding my life."

Monroe too was newly divorced, and she seems to have wanted nothing more than to marry Miller. In 1955 the screen siren had parted ways with her second husband, baseball legend Joe DiMaggio, with brutal criticism from the press. While Miller was collecting himself in Nevada, she was on location starring in the film *Bus Stop*. With Monroe being as complex as she was beautiful, Miller didn't know everything he *thought* he knew about her; he was unaware, for example, of her struggle with drug-dependency. During a phone call while she was shooting *Bus Stop*, Miller began to see the full picture, and it scared him. "Oh, Papa," Monroe cried breathlessly—her calling Miller "Papa" had begun as a joke but had stuck—"I don't want this anymore, Papa, I can't fight them alone, I want to live with you in the country and be a good wife...." Her weakness only endeared her to him: "I loved her as though I had loved her all my life; her pain was mine."

Miller and Monroe were married in June 1956—twice. After Monroe finished *Bus Stop*, they were secretly married in a civil ceremony. The judge didn't know that he was about to marry two of the most famous people in the United States, and certainly the most famous woman in the world. At the courthouse, Monroe appeared without the glamour that people had come to expect: without makeup, wearing a rumpled black skirt and pink sweater. Miller, next to her, wore a blue linen suit. They were impatient. They used their influence to get a waiver of the three-day waiting period and were married that evening in a five-minute ceremony. The groom borrowed a ring for the occasion.

The ceremony was not without dramatic tragedy: that night, Princess Mara Scherbatof, editor of the French magazine *Match*, died while pursuing the couple. She and an American photographer were following Miller and Monroe when the car swerved off a narrow, winding road and smashed into a tree, throwing her into the windshield. Miller acted quickly, sprinting to Scherbatof's car to help. He turned on his heels and bolted home to summon a doctor, but the woman died four hours later, in a hospital in New Milford, Connecticut.

The necessary second wedding was held for tradition. Monroe converted to Judaism, and Miller married her in a Jewish ceremony at the home of his longtime agent, Kay Brown. At the small gathering were Miller's parents, his brother and sister and their spouses, family friends the Rostens, and a rabbi. Marilyn was 30 years old, Miller 40. The marriage remained a secret for a few days before news broke, at which time it made front pages across the country.

THE HUAC

Miller was not yet free from controversy and the red scare. The very week of his marriage, the HUAC subpoenaed him to testify in Washington. Miller, having no other choice, appeared and listened as they questioned him. The HUAC wanted him to provide the names of colleagues he knew to be members of leftist organizations. "Whom did you see at a 1947 meeting of Communist writers in New York?" Just like his character John Proctor, Miller, asked to expose his friends, was faced with a moral decision.

Miller wrote later that what he witnessed firsthand was hypocrisy. In a country that had been formed with democratic principles, with freedom as a right for every citizen, here he was being interrogated about his beliefs. He refused to tell the HUAC anything at all and was charged with contempt—exactly what he was feeling. He faced imprisonment.

What is strange and ironic is Miller's true opinion about the ideals of the Communist Party. In his autobiography, *Timebends*, he says that American Communists were irrelevant. He did share many ideals of the Marxist movement, but the artist, as well as the man, was evolving from these positions. What he disliked, perhaps more than the idealism, was the notion that "power was forbidden to the individual and rightfully belonged to the collective," he wrote.

Still, whether Miller changed his views because of a deep soul searching or hindsight, when he was called back in 1957, his convictions still would not permit him to provide the names the Committee sought. During the hearing, he was truthful but not forthcoming. His passport to Belgium for the production of *The Crucible* had been denied; those believed to be Communist sympathizers, whether members of the Party or not, were often barred from traveling to help Communist causes abroad. Miller said that he couldn't remember supporting the Communist causes that the committee counsel had listed—but he also didn't deny that he had supported them. He was further questioned about his friend and professional collaborator Elia Kazan. When summoned to testify, Kazan admitted that he had been a Communist, and continued on to give the committee information on his friends and colleagues. When asked about his comments on Kazan's being an "informer," Miller denied the statement and said he had broken with Kazan for "personal reasons."

Miller admitted to having attended a meeting of the Communist Party but refused to reveal who else had been there. When asked whether artists had the right to advocate overthrow of the government, he responded, "this would be a desirable state of affairs." While Miller denied any affiliation with the Party, he added that he had misled them about his loyalty, that this was an error he had made "in all good faith because I was a very stupid man." He was eventually found guilty of contempt, fined $500, and sentenced to three months' probation. The judge asked him whether he desired to make a statement; Miller replied, "I do not, sir." Later, Miller issued a statement saying that he had "decided not to defend myself when I could have done otherwise because I did not believe, and I don't believe, that a man has to be an informer to practice his profession in the United States."

Meanwhile—while Miller's lawyers were busy keeping him out of jail—the London production of *A View from the Bridge* was reaping enthusiastic responses and good reviews. Monroe was working again, starring in a film, *The Prince and the Showgirl*, with stage and screen legend Laurence Olivier, whom she had met with Miller in England in 1956. Yet in the midst of all this confusion and goings on, Miller continued to work. A short story for the magazine *Esquire* that he called "The Misfits" proved to have as famous a history as any of his other works. In Miller's words, the story was about "our lives," their "meaninglessness," and "maybe how we got to where we are." It was a story that had his new wife's name written all over it.

THE PLAYWRIGHT AND THE MOVIE STAR

Miller the intellectual, the playwright, the man honored for his mind, represented everything Monroe craved. He saw something in her, something other than the image of the sex symbol: "It seemed to me that she could really be a great kind of phenomenon, a terrific artist." Still, he doubted the marriage early on. A friend commented that Miller seemed shocked to discover that Monroe was a human being, a person, and not an ideal. "We had both been let down from expectation such as few people allow themselves in marriage," he would later write in *Timebends*.

Monroe, a wife for the third time, began a normal life in the couple's rented home on Long Island. She learned to cook, she made homemade noodles, and the couple was settling in. This Monroe, one of so many, was domestic and caring, and Miller observed a new quietness, along with a new confidence.

While Monroe was under the care and supervision of a doctor, the doctor told her, at last, to expect the child she had longed for. Monroe was elated, but Miller, now in his forties, was apprehensive about becoming a father again. However, watching his wife embrace the idea of motherhood was touching and gave him hope. The hope didn't last long, though, as they learned that the baby wasn't growing correctly, and wouldn't survive. Monroe would require surgery.

Afterward, Miller, watching his wife grieving in the hospital, could think of no way to soothe her. A photographer friend, Sam Shaw, visited the hospital, and Miller talked to him about his wife. Monroe needed to understand her own power, Miller thought; there was something that a great role, the role of lifetime, would unleash in her. Shaw mentioned his *Esquire* story and suggested it as a film. It was a story that had a female role of the kind that comes once in a lifetime.

The artist in Miller saw the possibilities, and he began work on the screenplay. He spent entire days constructing a gift for Marilyn—a gift of art for the woman he considered a work of art. Miller was surprised at Marilyn's cool reaction to his suggestion that she play the lead character, Roslyn. She had read the script, and laughed at the cowboy parts, but would not commit to playing Roslyn. Miller was hurt, but he understood that ultimately the decision was hers.

He sent the finished screenplay to director John Huston, whom Monroe had worked with in the film *The Asphalt Jungle*. Huston was one of the first to detect true potential in her, and Monroe had never forgotten his kindness. In a town of bad memories, Huston was one of the few good ones left.

That Miller would tackle a Hollywood film was the ultimate compromise. Never before had he written a screenplay specifically for an actor; but the yearning to bond with Monroe—to make her fully realize his love and commitment, to cut through his guilt and bring her closer to him—was consuming him. His feeling that he never could understand his wife, her apprehensions, her mistrust of the world, made him all the more determined to prove his love. Huston agreed to direct the film and scheduled a meeting with Miller to go over the script.

More good news followed. By 1958, the shadow of the HUAC and Miller's contempt charges were now history. Miller was a footnote in the annals of the Hollywood blacklist that had marred the careers of so many men and women. The fate of others, like the Hollywood Ten—a group of screenwriters and directors who were barred from having their work made or, if made, credited to their names—would not befall Miller. The cloud had lifted enough for him to work. The ordeal had disgusted him, and he was glad to be rid of it. *The Misfits* was the creative passageway to the first project in years that he would undertake as a free artist.

But the film that had begun as a gift of love for his wife would leave their marriage in shambles. Before writing the screenplay, Miller had all but given up ever writing again. He was uneasy with Hollywood in general and with the collaborative nature of filmmaking in particular. Still, he wanted to devote himself totally to Monroe and to relieve her of her self-destructive tendencies. Miller had resigned himself to being a martyr; his work on the screenplay was an act of selflessness.

Monroe's character, Roslyn, was her first mature role as an actress, and Huston treated her like a professional. This woman, and the story of her, was close to Monroe, or what Miller wanted her to accept about herself. "It was far from accidental that by the end of the film Roslyn does find it possible to believe in a man and in her own survival," Miller wrote. His wife and her character had the same dilemma, but it was resolved only for the character.

Monroe's talent for forgetting and rephrasing the written lines didn't help the worsening *Misfits* situation. She began to revert to her former habits, appearing on the set later each day. Her exhaustion was showing in her close-ups, and it took her so long to get going in the morning that a crew member later recalled having to "make her up while she lay in her bed."

Miller watched as his wife was attended to by a physician from Los Angeles. Lying in bed, sick and distant, she was unaware of the fact that she was costing the production time and money. Miller, fearing for her life, felt useless, "like a bag of nails thrown in her face, a reminder of her failure to pull herself out of her old life even when she had at last truly loved someone." Miller has since recalled, "She was 'Marilyn Monroe' and that was what was killing her."

Huston, the proud, no-nonsense director, stepped in and had Monroe flown to a hospital in Los Angeles for treatment. Ten days later she was back on the set, looking wonderful again. She finished the film, and seemed relieved of a burden. However, she hardly spoke to Miller without causing him anguish. What the playwright had thought was the actress Monroe working through her character was identical to the cool, remote woman that shut him out. He realized that there were aspects of Monroe's depression and willful self-destruction that he would never understand. Neither his talent for penetrating character and motivation, nor his understanding of what made people tick, proved useful in understanding his own wife.

Clark Gable, the handsome actor who had made the character Rhett Butler of *Gone with the Wind* a Hollywood icon, starred opposite Monroe in *The Misfits*—although by this time, he was in his sixties and about to become a new father. When Gable saw the rough version of the film, he told Miller that it was the best work he had ever done as an actor. It would be Gable's last film; he died of a heart attack four days later.

Monroe was distraught at the news of her film idol's death. As a child, she had had the strange fantasy that Gable was her real father. She felt complicity and guilt over her behavior in his final days: "I kept him waiting. Hours and hours I kept him waiting on that picture!"

When the shoot was over and the final scene wrapped, the crew packed up and Huston hustled off to work on the editing. The screen version of Miller's story about alienation, isolation, the "meaning-lessness" of living, was finished, but Miller, who now felt shame at offering his private life for public entertainment, drifted away from his creation. Although the film received wide acclaim and is still considered among the cinematic greats, working on it had scarred many people.

Monroe had given a landmark performance. She rose, fell, and rose again to the challenge. For his part, Miller felt disheartened and taken for granted. Monroe had no concept, he thought, of the hours, days, and months of time he spent to hold her up by a thread that could snap at any minute. Without a word about it between them, Miller knew their separation was complete. Ironically, the filming in Nevada had placed Miller at the same spot outside Reno to which he had traveled four years earlier, when he had decided to leave Mary Slattery for Monroe.

He drove back alone to Los Angeles, the town of Monroe's birth, in his "clunky green American Motors mess." Miller would later write about his wife, the movie star, and set her as a character in a play that would find him assaulted in the press for indecency while he defended his right to write what he saw as the truth. The product, *After the Fall*, was quintessential Miller. He wrote: "The unstated question posed in *The Fall* was not how to live with a bad conscience ... but how to find out why one went to another's rescue only to help in his defeat by collaborating in obscuring reality from his eyes." This notion supports an idea he would express much later in his journals: "He who understands everything about his subject cannot write it. I write as much to discover as to explain." The theme of rescue and defeat was as fresh as the wounds of his marriage. For Miller, the tragedy he crafted for the stage would become the real-life horror he would live. The coincidences in Miller's art and life were striking, and perhaps not at all coincidental.

In January 1961, Monroe filed for divorce. Two months later Miller's 80-year old mother, Gussie, died. Two of the most prominent women in his life had left him, and all appeared to be on the brink of chaos and confusion. Writing became his sanctuary.

Not fully satisfied with *The Misfits*, Miller reworked the material, and expanded the short story into a novel. But it was another experience associated with *The Misfits* that Miller would carry into his future—while on location, Miller had met the woman who would become his third wife. Ingeborg Morath, a young Austrian photographer who traveled the world with the famed Henri Cartier-Bresson, had taken pictures of the production. She had previously photographed Huston's *The Unforgiven* and was admired by the director immensely. She was a confident and self-assured woman, with a slender, noble bearing—unlike Monroe in every way. Miller was attracted to her, but they had yet to discover what would become real love later. Their paths would cross again, and Miller would begin a new life, again. Like the mythical phoenix, Miller the artist was continually rising from the ashes of a world that kept burning down. His next works would put him in the spotlight as he hadn't been since *Death of a Salesman*.

FACING HISTORY

Miller felt a "hunger" to get back on his feet again as a writer. His frustration with the theater and with writing plays, in what he termed "a strange futility," weighed on him. He was at a place in his life where he had to find his way back to himself. In the early, tumultuous 1960s, however, the American theater was not receptive to the work of a moralist like Miller.

"I suppose the theater disgusted me," he recalls, "because it seemed merely a sordid ego exercise, nothing more, and I hated egotism now, my own no less than others'. The tradition that a play of any significance had to address the human destiny seemed ludicrously presumptuous." Yet not creating anything was worse.

Inge Morath was in his life by now, and painfully reminded of the ordeal with Monroe and the inescapable pain of that marriage, Miller was cautious—Miller had sworn that he would never marry again. Inge, with her purposeful way and talent and cheerful outlook, did not pressure him. Enjoying the company of a woman, an artist in her own right, was a revelation for him; in every way she was his equal. "I had been sure it would never come to me again," he wrote. But it did. With Inge, he found the need to "reach out and find the same person, to rely and be relied upon."

In 1962, Morath became his life partner, and their daughter, Rebecca, was born in September of the following year. His other children, Bob and Jane, were older now and doing well in their lives. Miller divided his time between two homes, one in Roxbury, Massachusetts, and an apartment in the Chelsea Hotel in Manhattan, a haunt for artists and writers. He was disillusioned about the theater, and this, his third marriage, to a busy talented photographer who was on assignment in Europe, left him alone much of the time. He was feeling apathetic, lonely, and unhappy, and he searched for something to write about.

Miller couldn't concentrate on any one topic for an extended period of time, and in looking back at this restless time, the playwright himself later agreed that even a seemingly humorous tale he wrote for film, *The Truth Drug*, was absurd. The scenario of a researcher who stumbles upon a drug called "Love" that, when ingested, changes aggressive, pushy people into loving, passive ones was left in a stack with other half attempts, collecting dust. He needed motivation, something to sink his teeth into, and he needed to prove that he still had it in him. The fragments of a story began to form an outline in his mind.

The story of the creation of the atom bomb had intrigued Miller since the end of World War II. The Manhattan Project—and the scientists who had built the top secret weapon, with the resulting catastrophic loss of life that occurred when the bomb was dropped on the people in Nagasaki and Hiroshima in 1945—had all the elements of a big story. He met with Hans Bethe, the man who designed a crucial part of the bomb—the lens—without which the bombs, named "Fat Man and Little Boy," could not explode. Miller hadn't a clue that he was about to write a different kind of play, one based on these real events.

Miller interviewed J. Robert Oppenheimer, the flamboyant genius who had led the team that developed the bomb, and other men directly involved. He wondered whether these men suffered from guilt over their creation. He wondered how a person working on something so grave and destructive could separate his work from his feelings about how it would be used. He wondered how one could become blind to the facts, and the playwright had his theme.

In his studio in Roxbury, Miller worked in a mad rush of energy. What he typed on the page was a long, unwieldy play written in blank verse, like a poem without end. He molded his main character on Oppenheimer, but the form didn't work, and the piece lacked a dramatic focus. He set it aside and set about the task of reshaping it. Somehow the idea of guilt wasn't fully formed; "guilt" alone was an insufficient premise.

He was stirred by another thought: How does one deny responsibility for one's own actions? On the other hand, "Why was one responsible if one had no evil intention?" Taking this line of reasoning further, Miller turned the question inside out: "If one had no evil intention, then where did the evil come from?"

During this time of philosophical contemplation, producer Robert Whitehead called upon Miller hoping to interest him in a theater project he was developing for the Lincoln Center. A new repertory company was forming that wanted to showcase work by prominent American writers. Miller was hand-picked to write the play that would be part of the grand opening.

The timing was fantastic. Miller would have a chance to work, after too many years of separation, with his old collaborators, Elia Kazan and Harold Clurman, from the Group Theatre. His relationship with Kazan had been strained since the HUAC hearings, and Miller still harbored distaste for Kazan's "moral defection." Yet Kazan's ability as a director was never questioned, and Miller believed that Kazan was the best man for the job. More than anything, however, Miller was worried whether or not he could complete the work in time. The play was still in rough shape, and Miller, the perfectionist, wanted it to be just right. He had two years to work on it.

In August 1962, as Miller was finishing the first version of *After the Fall*, he heard the same news that shocked the rest of the world: Marilyn Monroe was dead. She had, it was reported, taken an overdose of sleeping pills. Her apparent suicide shocked the nation, particularly as she may have been linked romantically to President Kennedy. Media coverage was relentless, and Miller could not escape it—no matter how bruised his own feelings were.

"There are people so vivid in life that they seem not to disappear when they die," he said. For weeks after her death, Miller had to force himself to accept the fact that Monroe was gone. "I realized that I still, even then, expected to meet her once more, somewhere, sometime, and maybe talk sensibly about all the foolishness we had been through," he wrote. His denial was earnest and sad. When a reporter called and asked whether he would be attending the funeral in California, Miller replied, "She won't be there." Such power did Monroe have over him that Miller believed that in meeting her once more he would fall in love with her again; Marilyn Monroe, "the saddest girl I've ever known."

His play was sitting idle, waiting for its author to breathe life into it. Despite the personal tragedy, he returned to work.

The next version of his drama benefited from a trip Miller took to Germany in 1964 to attend the trials of Nazi criminals held in Frankfurt. Morath was at his side as Miller, acting as a reporter, watched scene after scene of defendants admitting to unimaginable atrocities during the war. The testimony of the doctors and scientists who had examined the concentration camps after their liberation, as well as watching his wife Inge fight back tears, moved Miller beyond words.

The story of *After the Fall* suddenly had larger implications. The issues were more complex. How do "nations and individuals destroy ourselves by denying that this is precisely what we are doing?"

Miller wrote about the trials. As a special representative for *The New York Herald Tribune*, his article was published in the international edition. For the play, his duty now was to express, as well as he could, this "paradox of denial" he found in Germany. The country and the countrymen responsible for the murder of millions of Jews, the Holocaust that was irrational in its motives and monumental in its horror—these realities plunged Miller into a newfound commitment to get to the truth of his play. Miller embraced the challenge, and soon the play was ready.

Unfortunately, as his luck would have it, Miller's cycle of bad news continued. The Lincoln Center production was cancelled. Miller and producer Whitehead couldn't let the play wither away after all of the time and effort they had invested. They moved the play to a new repertory theater on West Fourth Street in New York. The building had a leaky roof, and on the day the play opened Miller and Whitehead were screwing bolts into the seats. It was like moving a production from a palace, like the Lincoln Center, to a one-room shack. The play was a miserable failure.

With rehearsals performed in secrecy, Miller wanted to seal the play from the outside world. "I don't want writers judging the play before it's been seen," he said. "That kind of thing stinks." But he couldn't control the climate—the next Arthur Miller play was to be a huge event, anticipated with the kind of expectations that only a play written by a man who was married to the fantasy girl of the world could incite. Before the actual premiere the play was being reviewed in the press and people rushed to the public previews. They wanted to see scandal, and they wanted the story of Miller's marriage to Monroe—there was no interest in the lofty themes Miller was exploring.

Miller was viciously attacked in the press. Critics held nothing back in attacking what they thought was a distasteful use of the now deceased Marilyn Monroe as the model for his character of Maggie—who died, as the movie star had, from an overdose of sleeping pills. The uncanny resemblance of Maggie to his former wife did not go unnoticed. One reviewer wrote that this play by the Pulitzer Prize–winning author seemed "torn from his life with the blood still on it." A prominent New York industrialist, Dr. John Myers, a personal friend of Monroe, wrote a press release to be published in the newspapers, calling Miller "a cruel, vain, contemptible human being," and scorning Miller for recounting "certain boudoir intimacies which no one has a right to reveal."

It was, to be sure, the most nakedly autobiographical play Miller had penned. The male character Quentin, in speeches about surviving a siege of despair, was instantly recognized as a stand-in for Miller. However, Miller was surprised by the outrage, although he later admitted that the play was doomed to fail, coming so soon after Monroe's death.

He denied bashing Monroe, defending his work and claiming that the critics had missed the overall theme. He summarized the story as "the trial of a man by his own conscience, his own values, and his own deeds." He answered his critics through his writing an article for *Life*, ten days after the opening. It blasted the cover with a bold headline: "Marilyn's Ghost: Arthur Miller Writes About His Shocking New Play." Miller titled his article, "With Respect for Her Agony—But with Love."

"That man up there isn't me," he said in a *Newsweek* interview. "A playwright doesn't put himself on the stage, he only dramatizes certain forces within himself." But Miller was pleading a cause he couldn't win.

Still, the similarities were too obvious to be ignored. The character Quentin, like Miller, was a child of the Depression. The "mother" resembled his dramatic real mother, and Quentin shared his life with three women, as Miller had. After a disastrous marriage, Quentin married an Austrian girl. When he explained that Maggie was "a character in a play about the human animal's unwillingness or inability to discover in itself, the seeds of its own destruction," few could believe that he wasn't referring to Monroe. With almost solemn reflection, Miller noted later, in the introduction to his *Collected Plays*, that "the intention behind a work of art and its effects upon the public are not always the same."

After such disappointment and anguish over his work and his life, Miller still found the strength to move past this experience. His reluctance to claim the theater as the place for his voice abated. Later he would say that the "theater may yet be one of the glories of the earth."

With the heat of *After the Fall* still swirling around him, Whitehead asked Miller for another play, one based loosely on a story of a friend, a psychoanalyst, who had been arrested in 1942 during a roundup of Jews in Vichy, France. The man was carrying false papers designed to prove that he wasn't Jewish when he took his place in line with others waiting to be questioned. Men would enter a door at the front of the line and not come back. When there was but one man between him and the door, his friend was certain that he would meet death. The door swung open, however, and the man who had entered before him handed his friend his own pass, telling him to go. A man he had never met and would not see again saved his friend. In the play, Miller kept the men from meeting and left the one wondering who had saved him.

Miller was able to use much of the information he had gathered while in Germany during the Nazi trials, and his viewpoint was sharpened. The tall, razor-thin Miller was 49 years old when he turned out the play in three weeks. When it went into production, only 20 lines were changed. Whereas he dealt with Nazism as a backdrop in *After the Fall*, it was the central topic in this play, *Incident at Vichy*.

Miller wrote this piece in an act of self-affirmation. "No matter what the reception of *Incident at Vichy* is, I'm satisfied that the play exists," he told *The New York Times* in 1964. "It very successfully does what I want it to do."

The play opened at New York's Anta Theater with performers from the Lincoln Center Repertory Company. With a cast of 17 men and playing from start to curtain without intermission, the production had an added advantage for Miller. Working with a group of young theater actors without profit motivations made it an example of something he had missed: art theater.

Incident at Vichy was his ninth play. It was banned in the Soviet Union. The French followed suit, not directly banning the play but preventing it from being produced by three interested parties.

Underlying this action was the fear that audiences might take the play's plot twist personally. Within the simple story line is the implication, stated or not, that the French collaborated with the Nazis and their anti-Semitism.

In 1964, many were still sensitive to subtle accusations of having contributed to the genocidal practices of the Nazis. Offstage, Miller's themes of denial and guilt were played out, as the work would not be produced in Paris until the 1980s. In the end, despite all the years that had passed between, the play was criticized in France, and its run ended.

"I have often rescued a sense of reality," Miller wrote, "by recalling Chekov's remark: 'If I had listened to the critics I'd have died drunk in the gutter.'" Out of the past, the words of a Russian playwright from another century secured Miller's faith in himself. Then, as Miller and his wife were in Paris, attending Luchino Visconti's production of *After the Fall*, he received a phone call from London. David Carver, president of Poets, Essayists, and Novelists (PEN), an international writers' association, wanted to meet with him. Carver was hoping Miller would become president of PEN's international congress. Miller had never heard of this organization. Exceptional literary figures, like playwright George Bernard Shaw and writer H.G. Wells, had founded the group after World War I. Their mission was to work for freedom of expression and to battle censorship. Carver explained to Miller that PEN had helped to convince the Hungarian government to release imprisoned writers after the Russian invasion of 1956. It was a cause Miller could align himself with, but he didn't quite comprehend why Carver wanted him.

PEN needed a prominent name, Carver explained, a writer with a political conscience who would lend the group international attention. They needed an image-maker, a leader. Miller seemed perfect to them, but he was still unsure: "I had a suspicion of being used." With his political track record, he honestly thought this could be a ploy by the Central Intelligence Agency (CIA). So, to flush them out, he asked Carver what he would think if he invited some Soviet writers to join PEN. Carver was floored. The Cold War had caused friction between the East and West, and the gesture might work to heal old wounds and form better relationships.

After a few days of thinking it over, Miller decided to accept the presidency. In his initial public forum as president, the author was in Bled, Yugoslavia, for the organization's first international congress. Within days he was giving speeches and planning upcoming conferences. It would be the work that would lead him into the next phase of his life, one that would include fighting for the rights of writers around the world. His personal experience of censorship and intimidation during the HUAC era was still fresh in his memory, and this position was a way to correct wrongs and to make a lasting impact for writers.

By this time, Miller's works had found their way into new markets. *Incident at Vichy* was published in book form, and two of his major works, *Death of a Salesman* and *The Crucible*, were produced for television. Miller also explored other venues—a collection of short stories, "I Don't Need You Anymore," appeared in 1967. About his role with PEN, Miller wrote of the time that, "Willy-nilly, I was pitched into the still indeterminate tangle of détente politics to begin a new and totally unexpected stage of my learning life."

MESSAGE PLAYS

Two estranged brothers, a policeman and a surgeon, meet years later after an angry parting, pulled together only through the death of their father. With the brothers sorting through the family's possessions and dividing the property, the past transgressions intrude, old feelings resurface, and without peace or forgiveness they part yet again. In the end, they sell the family's heirlooms to an 80-year-old furniture dealer.

This was the premise for Miller's play *The Price*, a family drama with themes he had visited in his previous works. In the playwright's mind, when people do not face the truth, tragedy is born. In a sense, this has become a dramatic "law" for the inhabitants of his plays. The ideas should be easily grasped: "A play ought to make sense to common-sense people," he later wrote. "The only challenge worth the effort is the widest one and the tallest one, which is the people themselves."

The production problems that were by now routine in staging a Miller play left a mark on this one too. The cast argued with director Ulu Grosbard, who had conflicts with everyone. The production was seriously in trouble and was stopped in its tracks when three actors almost quit after a fight with Grosbard. After this the director was asked to resign. During previews in Philadelphia, Miller took on the role of director, just as he had with *The Crucible*. Miller did not want to lead the play as a director—he was a writer, first and foremost, and he did not enjoy directing his own work. Still, he had to save the play, and thus he took the reins.

But a new dilemma arose. Forty-eight hours before the show's opening, a lead actor was rushed to the hospital to have an operation for a "kinked" colon. There was no choice but to replace him with the understudy, who gave a surprisingly good performance. Later, the cast and crew would hear a singular story about the rehabilitated actor: While working in a different production, their former leading man delivered a comic line that made the audience roar with laughter—and then collapsed and died on stage, the crowd still applauding.

When *The Price* opened on Broadway in 1968, no one knew that it would become one of Miller's longest-running plays. It didn't close until a year and 425 performances later. Then, in March 1968, 20 years after its groundbreaking (if mixed) debut, was sold the millionth copy of *Death of a Salesman*. Miller had become a playwright of the people.

He was more than famous now. He was popular, a playwright who was a household name. In the 1960s, Miller's early "realistic" play was competing with an audience captivated by the "experimental," but it still held up. By the late 1960s, *Death of a Salesman* had entered the league of timeless works of art in an age that was using a new definition of "art." The age was, in fact, redefining everything.

When the time came for the nation to elect a new president, Miller was nominated as a delegate to represent Connecticut at the 1968 Democratic National Convention, to be held in Chicago. Miller was not particularly enthusiastic about the changes in his country. He "saw the seeds of a coming new disillusionment" and felt that America was being ripped apart. He had written and spoken out against the Vietnam War, but at the age of 50 it was "echoes of past crusades," impossible to ignore. "The sixties was a time of stalemate for me," he recalled later. "Perhaps because I had lost the last belief in any social prophecy. I could find no refreshing current of history such as I had imagined touching in the thirties and forties, only a moral stagnation that mocked creation itself."

In a mournful lament about the rise in crime and the Vietnam War, a thoughtful Miller wrote, "Few people even begin to imagine that they might have some symbolic or even personal connection with this violence." It was a thorny subject, and Miller could not fathom this disconnection. He questioned himself and others. Was it "possible to say convincingly that this destruction of an ethic also destroys my will to oppose violence in the streets?" Miller the artist and observer couldn't shy away from his own mixed feelings and thought that others should face their attitudes truthfully as well.

The week Miller spent in Chicago in 1968 became the climax of a decade of turmoil. Outside the convention center, students raged and were beaten by the police, as television networks broadcasted footage of the violence. The city had come unhinged. Miller described a scene: "Helmeted troops stood with rifles in a long line facing Grant Park across Michigan Avenue, where in the darkness one could make out a camping mass of the young, quiet now after the day's beatings and arrests." Douglas Kiker, an NBC reporter who had been in Budapest in 1956, when the Russians had plowed through the streets, commented to Miller that this was the most frightening display of violence he had ever witnessed.

There was no peace inside the halls. When Senator Abraham Ribicoff, former Governor of Connecticut, took the podium to speak, Miller saw Chicago Mayor Richard Daley make a cutting motion across his throat with his index finger, yelling "Jew! Jew!" The playwright, with more than 30 years of experience in the theater, had been both a player and audience member in a surreal drama of chaos and hopelessness. This theater of politics left him empty.

Soon, though, with his own brand of fire and conviction, his life of politics and art would mesh more completely. There were larger problems in the world, and there had to be a way to address them and start a dialogue. As the president of PEN, Miller could enact changes. He became the advocate of free expression and took on a bold assignment by lending his name and support to a blacklisted Russian author.

Miller knew that the conditions for Soviet writers were deplorable, and that censorship was common. In his own words, he was annoying the Soviets with his protests. In 1968 he petitioned the government about novelist Aleksandr Solzhenitsyn. Solzhenitsyn had bravely written several books exploring the tyranny of his country. His *The Gulag Archipelago* was written as a first-person account of his incarceration and torture in the Soviet penal system under the dictator Stalin. "For several decades ... people were arrested who were guilty of nothing," Solzhenitsyn wrote. There was no limit to the evil, and those who went insane in the prison were executed.

It was a story that had never been told, and his work, like Miller's *Incident at Vichy*, was banned. Two years after Miller's petition on behalf of Solzhenitsyn, the Soviet Union banned all of Miller's work.

It seemed impossible that Miller, who had made inroads with the Soviet writers at the PEN conference in Bled, Yugoslavia, convincing them of the importance of their involvement, could be the object of a total ban. When the head of the Soviet delegation, writer Alexei Surkov, grumbled to him during the last night of the conference that the Soviets were ready and wanted to join PEN if changes could be made in the constitution to accommodate them, Miller was confident he had allies. A year later, he was in Moscow talking to Surkov.

Before his trip, he sent endless wires and letters to Surkov protesting the treatment of the Lithuanians and Estonians, as well as the Russians, and was able to secure exit visas for some. He wrote about the repression of Jews. But his monumental achievement was tarnished with the ban of his art.

Miller's idealism was not deflected long. PEN was an international force that would act as the conscience of the world writing community. "In a word, literature had to speak to the present condition of man's life and thus would implicitly have to stand against injustice as the destroyer of life." Miller used the power of his position, and a newfound respect for the organization emerged.

One day he received a telegram from London about Nigerian writer Wole Soyinka. Miller knew little about the poet and playwright, except that he was in danger of being executed. Soyinka was a known political activist and had volunteered himself as negotiator between the Biafran people and the Nigerian government. Soyinka wanted to help stop the bloody civil war that was tearing his country apart. A letter arrived for the president of PEN: could Miller get a message to General Gowan, commander of the army, and ask him to spare Soyinka's life? Miller enlisted the help of friends and contacted the general with a formal request to reconsider Soyinka's case. When the general saw Miller's name, he asked whether it was the same Miller who had been married to Marilyn Monroe. On learning that this was true, he immediately released Soyinka.

Having been tried in the 1950s for his staunch resistance to censorship or control of any author's work, Miller had intimate knowledge of the consequences of standing up to authority. It was gratifying to use his influence as a playwright to promote freedom of ideas and to make a difference in the lives of others. There was purpose and meaning to his life beyond writing plays. Although writing was fulfilling, to strive to liberate other writers was to declare a profound kinship with members of a tribe scattered in countries around the globe.

When Miller refused to allow his work to be sold in Greece as an act of solidarity with that country's oppressed writers, governments the world over were put on the spot. An unjust system was brought to light and was symbolically placed on trial by an outspoken leader for the right to write. People had to respond one way or the other.

Miller was a tireless campaigner for correcting a moral wrong when he saw one. A situation close to home would offer him the chance for another victory against injustice.

In 1973 he had his hands on a copy of a *New York Times* article about an 18-year-old New Canaan man named Peter Reilly who had confessed to murdering his mother. The transcriptions of a Connecticut state police interrogation of the teenager alarmed Miller. Reilly had been wrongfully convicted, a letter explained. Would Miller help?

The town residents were sure of the young man's innocence—so sure that many were mortgaging their homes and donating their savings to pay for a new trial. When Miller discovered that Reilly had confessed to the murder after 10 straight hours of interrogation and went without legal counsel for 24 hours, he suspected fraud. He read on with anger. Incredibly, at the end of the emotionally draining session, a mentally broken and confused Reilly asked his accusers if they were really sure that he was the killer. They told him that they were sure. The weeping Reilly signed the confession. After one night of rest he retracted all of it, but the damage was done.

For the next five years, Miller worked to free the convicted youth, helping to form a solid case that would overturn his conviction. With the unflagging assistance of private investigators and lawyers, they found eyewitnesses who had seen Reilly on the night of his mother's murder—five miles from his home. The witnesses were a local police officer and his wife.

It was worse than Miller could have imagined. The couple had already given a statement to the police about Reilly's whereabouts. The affidavit was lost in the files of the prosecuting attorney. He knew and the truth, with full knowledge of Reilly's innocence, had convicted Reilly anyway, the real murderer to walk the streets.

Miller brought in a criminal pathologist, Dr. Milton Helpern, to examine the evidence. Helpern's conclusion: it was impossible that Reilly could have committed the murder described without leaving a speck of blood on his clothes or body.

Reilly was eventually cleared of all charges. "If the long months of the Reilly case left a darkened picture of man," the author reasoned, "it was no less perplexing for being accompanied by the most unlikely examples of courage and goodness." The investigator and lawyer worked for almost nothing.

The playwright found the ordeal depressing and, during this time, used his calling as an artist to write a new play about human nature. *The Creation of the World and Other Business* was a conversation about God and how He was created. In the play, man is declared guilty, despite the fact that it is God the Almighty who argues for him.

The theme and stylization were radical departures for Miller. He made a break with pure realism and worked the ideas within the framework of a fantasy. Miller was still searching for innovative ways to tell a story. He took risks even when the work didn't garner the attention he wanted. The nervousness he sometimes felt at starting a play kept him company year after year.

"I'm writing a play—God, why do I do it, when I think what lies ahead?" he told an interviewer. "Why don't I write prose? It's about the chaos, I guess. It's telling me bit by bit what it is. Ideas come from some process of paradox and irony, some contradictory thing."

The child of the Depression had traveled far from his days in Harlem. The circle of his life expanded to include the world and then, in 1973, swung full circle, back to his beginnings. His old Alma Mater, the University of Michigan, made the playwright their professor in residence. The school that had given him the Hopwood Award, his first prize for a dramatic work, was giving him another honor. It was at this campus where he had met his first wife, Mary Slattery, and where he realized that "a play was entwined with my very conception of myself" and that he would "never write anything good that did not somehow make me blush."

There would be more recognition from universities to follow, and more plays written, and television was on a Miller mission again.

In 1974 the play that had caused the press and fans alike to launch personal attacks against the writer was produced as a television movie.

Ten years later some of the smoke had cleared and Americans could watch on the small screen a play that would forever be tied to Marilyn Monroe: *After the Fall*.

It was all a part of his past, and in the next decade he would write down his life in a thick memoir. "Over the next years I would become more and more deeply absorbed by a kind of imploding of time— moments when a buried layer of experience suddenly surges upward to become the new surface of one's attention and flashes news from below." Time, life, and art were about to implode for Miller. He was about to throw himself headlong into the dangerous world of a diplomat.

MIRROR OF LIFE

"A character is defined by the kinds of challenges he cannot walk away from," Miller wrote in his journal. "And by those he has walked away from that cause him remorse." It's almost as if he's staring into a mirror and writing down what he sees in himself. His entire life is a reflection of those words. Miller the playwright was describing how to create strong characters for theater, people that were at the crossroads of a moral choice in their lives. "Great drama is great questions or it is nothing but technique," he reminds us.

In all of Miller's work, he places his characters at a fork in the road: Joe Keller in *All My Sons*, John Proctor in *The Crucible*, Eddie Carbone in *A View from the Bridge*. The playwright himself, just like his characters, came to yet another turning point, and he had to choose what he would stand for and what he would walk away from.

In the 1970s Miller decided that he would not turn his back on causes that people found unpleasant, that could make him the object of angry threats and ridicule. Israel, a place with a history of struggle for peace and independence, held beauty and despair for Miller. The world hadn't purged itself of anti-Jewish feelings, and the Israelis were caught in a no-win situation. Miller went public with his denouncement of the United Nations and how it treated Israel. Its policies were unfair, he claimed, and they were the cause of Israel's misery.

Miller was like a steamroller—he protested the treatment of writers in Iran, and he appeared on a panel before the United States Senate to urge them to support freedom of writers around the world. He also participated in a symposium on Jewish culture and Jewish writers, and a letter of protest to be forwarded to the Czech head of state to protest oppression of Czechoslovakian writers got an Arthur Miller endorsement.

Miller was still concerned for writers less fortunate than he was and passionate about opening doors for artists the world over. He did not stop speaking out for writers even after he was no longer president of PEN. He would always lend his voice as a delegate. One such mission took him to the land of Turkey for an international PEN conference where at dinner, a writer sitting next to Miller told him, "If they arrest me I will escape the country. I could not face torture like that again." The persecution these writers spoke about to him was real—they were fighting for their very lives.

As a delegate at a meeting of Soviet and American writers in Lithuania, he repeated a decades-old plea. Would the Soviets please stop persecuting writers? Could they stop, please! When the Soviet Union began to open up to outsiders, Miller was invited in 1986 to a conference, at which he met a Soviet leader who stressed a "new thinking": an invitation came to meet with the new president Mikhail Gorbachov. What Miller thought would be a 10-minute introduction turned into nearly three hours of candid discussion on Soviet policies. After years of petitions and conferences and promises, this was change.

In the 1970s, Miller was identified as more than just a playwright. He was an artist who appealed to social causes, and his next plays would be a collection of dramatic works that were directly influenced by his close encounters in the political realm.

The Archbishop's Ceiling, written from his experience as president of PEN, in Prague, Czechoslovakia, deals with the Soviet Union's mistreatment of dissident writers. It was tuned up for the stage in 1977 and produced in New Haven, Connecticut, before moving to Washington, D.C. The play, along with *The American Clock*, a series of dramatic vignettes based on Studs Terkel's book *Hard Times*, didn't do as well as his other work. In Miller's words, the plays were "hard-minded attempts to grasp what I felt life in the seventies had all but lost—a unified concept of human beings." Broadway wasn't taking too many risks. Intellectual plays were competing with pure entertainment.

Yet it's almost a tradition of the later Miller plays that they receive lukewarm reception and then burst on the scene later to reap the bounty. Ten years after their American premieres, *The Archbishop's Ceiling* and *The American Clock* were filling theater houses in London.

"A play, even the angry and critical kind, is always on one level a love letter to the world, from which loving acknowledgment is eagerly awaited," he wrote. This time, that "loving acknowledgment" came from China. Miller and his wife had combined their lives and their art. They began working on projects together, with Miller as the writer and the books laced with Inge's wonderful photographs. This marriage had blossomed into a partnership they both found fulfilling and cherished. They were devoted to each other, and this stability gave Miller a new kind of creative freedom. Inge was as fearless as he was, and anything was possible—China was possible.

Under Communist rule, China was a country sealed off from the world. Under the rulership of Mao, the Chinese had lived without much contact with foreigners. "No one of my generation can be understood without reference to his relation to Marxism as 'the God that failed,'" Miller wrote. His reference point was about to expand tremendously.

When Miller and his wife traveled to China in 1978, both were stunned at what they found. Few Westerners had seen the fall-out of the Cultural Revolution. China seemed suspended in time; the Mao era still held everyone in its tight grip—the artists and writers affected no less than others. Miller didn't know much about China before he arrived, and what he knew he soon realized was closer to fiction. He never expected to find the remnants of Communism moving among the people like a ghost.

"It was a hard shock to learn that every one of the two dozen or more writers, stage and film directors, actors, and artists we met in the first week of our stay had been either imprisoned or exiled to some distant province to feed pigs or plant rice, for as long as twelve years, and they were a mere handful out of thousands," he reported with regret. The book of their journey, *Chinese Encounters*, was published with Inge's photographs in 1979.

A couple of years after, while in Beijing, Miller met a woman who told him how one of his plays told a characteristically Chinese story, one that was only whispered about. The woman, writer Nien Cheng, told him she had spent six and one-half years in prison, in solitary confinement. After her release, she saw a production of *The Crucible* in Shanghai in 1980. She was astonished to learn that a non-Chinese person had written the play. The interrogation tactics were nearly identical as the ones used during the Cultural Revolution. To think that a play about Salem witches in 1692, inspired from Miller's experience of the witch-hunts of the 1950s, had translated to a Chinese experience he never knew existed was mind-boggling. Miller wrote in *Timebends* that he could not imagine a theater that did not want to change the world.

For some reason, Miller found a greater reception for his larger themes and the adaptations of his plays in television rather than in Hollywood films. In 1979 he wrote the teleplay *Playing for Time*, a tragedy about a woman who survived the Nazi death camps by performing in an all-prisoner musical group. The Nazis used this orchestra to soothe the prisoners marching to the gas chambers. Based on a memoir of Fania Fenelon's of an actual women's orchestra in Auschwitz, the film, starring Vanessa Redgrave, was a haunting look at the lives of Jews during the Holocaust.

Miller was being showered with awards. In 1984 he and Inge were awarded honorary doctorate degrees from the prestigious University of Hartford. Then, one year before the acceptance speeches, the couple was in China once more, this time for a production that Miller savors as one of the most thrilling events in his life. The People's Art Theater in Beijing, China, wanted to mount *Death of a Salesman*.

A younger Arthur Miller, writing on a 13-year-old secondhand portable typewriter in a marathon session that brought him to tears, was creating what would become a landmark event in the People's Republic of China. "I did not know that in 1948 in Connecticut that I was sending a message of resurgent individualism to the China of 1983." The theater troupe wanted Miller to direct, and this time Miller was ecstatic about the thought. It was the first production by the People's Art Theater by a foreign director in post-Mao China—an honor beyond words.

How would the Chinese relate to the character of Willy Loman? Miller realized that there was nothing about the play the Chinese didn't relate to: "The Chinese might disapprove of his lies and his self-deluding exaggerations as well as his immorality with women, but they certainly saw themselves in him." In the author's words, "Willy" was represented everywhere, in every kind of system. There was a universal quality about him that cut through cultural, class, and religious differences. After the performance, a young Chinese student told a CBS interviewer how the Chinese could understand such an American play: "We are moved by it because we also want to be number one, and to be rich and successful."

The cast was a marvel, and Miller insisted that they dress as they normally would, not disguise their "Chinese-ness" with wigs and makeup. The idea took some getting used to. Theater in China had little connection with regular people. Something so simple seemed radical.

Inge proved indispensable on this trip. Not only was she a gifted photographer; she also had an uncanny knack, a "genius," Miller has called it, for languages. When they made their first trip to Russia, Inge learned the language before they left. She was also fluent in English, French, Spanish, and Italian. When they had been in Greece for two weeks, on their last evening, Miller realized that she was speaking *that* language, too. During a luncheon in China, Inge found herself translating simultaneously for a German-speaking Chinese official, a Russian-speaking Chinese writer, and an English-speaking Chinese tourist.

Miller wrote *Salesman in Beijing*, a book about the two months he spent in China directing *Death of a Salesman*, and Inge's pictures documented everything. The play itself was published in Beijing in 1984, and the Beijing production gave Miller a deeper understanding of his work. He discovered more about what he thought he had already "explained."

Also in 1984, the Kennedy Center gave Miller a Lifetime Achievement Award. A revival of *Death of a Salesman* lit the stage in New York. "I have gone through years when my plays were being performed in half a dozen countries but not in New York," Miller has written. "Thus, when George Scott performed in *Salesman* in New York and Tony LoBianco in *A View from the Bridge* on Broadway, and then Dustin Hoffman in *Salesman* again ... I seemed to have been 'revived' when in fact I had only been invisible in my own land."

Starring actors Dustin Hoffman and John Malkovich, *Death of a Salesman* was a smash hit. Twenty years earlier, the promising young Hoffman had played the role of Willy's son Biff in a record album of the play, with the burly first Willy Loman, Lee J. Cobb. Now Hoffman himself was playing the salesman. Hoffman was a perfectionist known for totally engrossing himself in a character. In heavy makeup to make him look like an aging, balding man, he was the "shrimp" that Miller had originally envisioned. A year later, a broadcast of the production aired on CBS to an audience of 25 million.

In 1986 the British production of *The Archbishop's Ceiling* opened at the same time as the television version of Miller's first hit, *All My Sons*, and two one-act plays, *Clara* and *I Can't Remember Anything*, were produced at the Mitzi E. Newhouse Theater in Lincoln Center under the title *Danger: Memory!* In *Clara*, Kroll's murdered daughter aids his memory during interrogation, accompanied by giant images from a slide projector; *I Can't Remember Anything* concerns two elderly characters who struggle with memory lapses. Miller was nervous and predicted that the critics wouldn't understand the plays.

They didn't, but the letters he received from young writers who found this structure of storytelling "cutting-edge" encouraged him. "They understood," Miller wrote of the reaction to *Clara*, "that I had cast off absolutely every instrumentality of dramas except the two essential voices of the interrogating detective and Kroll."

In 1987, Miller published his long-awaited memoir—*Timebends: A Life*, a mountain of a book spanning his entire life and work. He was 72 years old and had been working in the theater for more than 40 years and had written a dozen plays. He wrote the book to correct some wrongs, too. Miller would hear stories about events said to have involved him—stories full of holes and sometimes not even truthful. He reasoned that a century from his autobiography's publication it may prove useful: "If there's any paper left unburned, someone picking up this book might get a clue of what life was like in the period that I've lived."

Critics hailed *Timebends* as an autobiography of the highest order. In an interview with *Life*, which published an extended excerpt, Miller says that he probably "would never have written this book had I not come upon a form in which I found it so pleasurable to compose."

The form is innovative, a way to tell his entire story at once. It isn't written in strict chronological order; instead, as the title suggests, time is bent on a curve, sometimes a circle, jumping forward and backward, weaving the past and present much the way he did in *Death of a Salesman*. As he meant to do with Willy Loman, Miller gives the public a look "inside his head"; in one way or another, everything is about making stories. "We were all mythmaking creatures, it seemed," he recalls, "who created not only art but lives no less fictional, no less willed into existence, if only we knew it."

LIFE AS A LEGEND

"I aspired," Miller has said, "to a rather exalted image of the dramatist as a species of truth-revealing leader." He has lived up to his aspirations, creating a corpus of significant art for the theater. His *An Enemy of the People* was produced for television and aired on PBS in 1990; time had dulled memories of the Hollywood blacklist, and at last Miller's craft could shine through. That same year saw the film *Everybody Wins*, based on his 1982 play *Some Kind of Love*, whose characters are left with the anguish of making decisions that they know are not based on truth. Miller was putting his characters through more difficult trials, and the realism was more layered, mixed with an understructure of feelings and emotions that the characters had to bring to the surface and deal with.

"The desire to move on, to metamorphose—or perhaps it is a talent for being contemporary—was given to me as life's inevitable and rightful condition." This urge to reinvent himself took 10 years of work for *The Ride Down Mount Morgan*, his eighteenth play—a comedy about a man who slams his Porsche into a snowy mountainside and ends up in the hospital, visited by two women, both married to him, and unaware of each other. The situation is uncharacteristic for him. "Inevitably," Miller explains in his autobiography, "the form of a new play was that of a confession, since the main character's quest for a connection to his own life was the issue, his conquest of denial the path into himself."

The Ride Down Mount Morgan opened in London. Robert Fox, its producer, said that when he got the play and read it, "It didn't remind me of anything else—I was just knocked over by how wonderfully well he writes, and how funny he is." Others have shared the opinion; England has reserved a special place for Miller's work, and Miller, over 80 years old, still captures honors and the popular imagination. He received the Mellon Bank Award for lifetime achievement in the humanities, and his novella *Homely Girl* was released in 1992.

Miller's following in England and Europe has always softened the blows of his topsy-turvy career in the American theater. The 1960s, for example, had been difficult: "For one thing, nobody seemed to want to hear a story anymore," he wrote. "A story, I theorized, meant some continuity from the past to the present, and in our gut we knew there was no such continuity in life where absolutely anything was perfectly possible for every kind of character."

Miller revised *The Ride Down Mount Morgan* for its American premiere in Williamstown, Massachusetts, before moving it to Broadway in 1997. When his next new work appeared on Broadway, Miller had been absent from The Great White Way for 14 years. The germ of the idea for *Broken Glass* came to Miller through an incident from 1937. He was a student at the University of Michigan at that time and had just bought a radio. By coincidence, he turned it on one night and received a transmission from Europe. He heard screaming, and he knew enough German to understand what was going on: he was listening to Hitler broadcasting a speech. "It was, historically, the hour when this whole thing exploded with the first incredible viciousness," he told *The Los Angeles Times*.

Broken Glass is the story of an American Jewish marriage falling apart in Brooklyn during *Kristallnacht*, November of 1938, "the night of broken glass." On that night in Germany, the Nazis went on a rampage, terrorizing Jews, setting fire to synagogues, and smashing store windows. In the play, a woman reads of the rising anti-Semitic violence in Europe and suffers a hysterical paralysis in her legs; the couple lives through the pain of a crumbling marriage and the horror of the fate of Jews at once distant and close to their hearts.

"This play should make Jewish and non-Jewish audiences ask what is in the soul that allows such things as the Holocaust to happen," Miller told *The Jewish Bulletin* in 1996. Plays so serious-minded as Miller's find more enthusiastic audiences abroad, Miller thinks, because theater in America does not value work that puts the audience ill at ease. But for Miller, the mission of the theater has always been sacred: "Theater was a kind of temple in which you were searching for redemption."

This does not mean that Miller has approved of all the incarnations that have been proposed for his work. When the idea of filming *The Crucible* was raised, for example, he couldn't imagine a more disagreeable venture; but his family wanted to be involved, particularly his son Robert. Robert Miller—who bears a remarkable physical resemblance to his father both in his lanky, tall frame and intense eyes—had had an uneven career in Hollywood when he asked his father for a chance to work on *The Crucible*. The senior Miller had warned his son that Hollywood was a wasted effort; but Robert's career was in the movie business, and he wanted to show his father that Hollywood did not *have* to be so negative an experience as it had been before.

The senior Miller remained skeptical—Hollywood had not been good to him. He was afraid of seeing another play on the big screen that made him want to run from the theater. Robert persisted, however, writing letters to his father, trying to sell the idea. Finally, after several years, Robert won his father's interest, and they agreed to make the attempt.

Working together brought father and son closer. Their relationship had been strained and difficult since Miller had left Robert's mother, Mary Slattery, to marry Marilyn Monroe, but Robert, now a grown man, was drawn to his father's work. The scenes of betrayal and forgiveness so key in *The Crucible* particularly moved him, and he felt he could understand his father better now than ever before.

Robert next had to convince Hollywood of the worth of a film version of *The Crucible*. He faced many objections and criticism. He even faced people who agreed to let him produce the film if his father wasn't attached as the screenwriter. The film was made, though, and received as a critical success. In addition, it brought a son-in-law into the Miller family: during the filming, dashing actor Daniel Day-Lewis—whose father, Cecil Day-Lewis, was a poet—was smitten by Miller's daughter Rebecca, and the pair dated secretly for a year and then announced their plans to marry.

Miller's newest creative ventures have met with increasingly warm receptions; his rightful place as America's greatest living playwright is being recognized all over again in the new millennium. *Broken Glass* was honored with the Olivier Award in 1995, while Oxford University gave Miller an honorary doctorate degree, and he received the William Inge Festival Award for his distinguished achievement in American theater—a timely gift for his 80th birthday. In 1998 came more accolades, including the Pell Award; Miller also has been named the Distinguished Inaugural Senior Fellow of the American Academy in Berlin and given a special Tony Award for lifetime achievement. In 1999, he received the Dorothy and Lillian Gish Prize, given to those who have had a significant impact on the American arts, which includes a silver medallion and a monetary award of about $200,000. Past honorees of the Gish Prize, which was established in the early 1990s, include singer/songwriter Bob Dylan and director Ingmar Bergman.

Arthur Miller has been a resilient force in the American theater for half a century. By 1999, *Death of a Salesman*, Miller's most enduring play, had sold more than 11 million copies and was being produced and acted *somewhere* in the world on almost every day of the year. *Salesman's* fiftieth birthday came in that same year, and it was revived, again, on Broadway. In an interview after receiving the Gish Prize, Miller himself summarized his rich creative life with hope, satisfaction, and an expressed desire to find continued support from his colleagues in the arts: "After a veritable lifetime given to writing plays, it is a great honor to receive this recognition from such distinguished participants in the arts.... I hope that the work I have still to do will reflect their kind and generous judgment."

NEIL HEIMS

Arthur Miller: An Introduction

I

The focus of Arthur Miller's work throughout his career has been the drama of people caught in the workings of history, and especially the conflicts which arise from the interplay of individual freedom and historical determinism. His plays pose such questions as what it means to be human, where the boundaries of responsibility lie, and what life is like when two contradictory forces both have power. In Miller's view, people are shaped by social, political, and economic circumstances and, at the same time, can draw on something from within and shape those circumstances.

Speaking in 1985 of *Death of a Salesman*, Miller said, "There's been a lot of writing and a lot of discussion in the last thirty-five years about man in society. We no longer think of people being abstracted, simply self-made. We realize now far more that the society's got a tremendous amount of input into our situation." (Blackwood)

The tension between "society's input" and "our situation" is what Miller's plays continually negotiate. Thus, although his plays are concerned with social issues and suggest values traditionally associated with leftist social ideals, they are never old-fashioned Communist-style vehicles of the sort that Clifford Odets could write. Neither are they metaphysical forays into the realms of contemporary personality that seem to dominate the work of playwrights like Eugene O'Neill, Tennessee Williams, or Edward Albee—*pace* Miller's keen interest in the psychology of people struggling to maintain their personal integrity within, and despite, history.

Even though Miller's plays reflect and express his political concerns and commitments and his lifelong activism, they are not "political" plays, but dramas of human experience set in the contexts of social, economic, and morally defining challenges. His plays are meditations on, and maps of, the intersection of imperfect individuals facing unjust circumstances. The plays also celebrate the struggles and, repeatedly, the sacrifices that grow out of that encounter to maintain something like humanity. Miller is a dramatic moralist and is always striving in his plays to probe and to prod, following in the tradition of two of his models, Henrik Ibsen and George Bernard Shaw.

Both of Miller's most famous and most frequently mounted plays, *Death of a Salesman* (1949) and *The Crucible* (1952), are dramas that trace the intersection of character and society. Willy Loman, the salesman who can no longer sell himself in *Death of a Salesman*, is a conformist. He has fashioned himself according to the values and images of "success." His economic and psychological circumstances make his existence so tenuous that he keeps awareness of how deeply at bay he is by inflating himself and "thinking positively."

Willy ignores reality and speaks as if his wish were already accomplished; he is caught in an illusion of himself and spreads his illusion among the members of his family. He instills in his sons the same tendency to build castles in the air. In particular, he teaches his son Biff that he is better than the other boys, a leader, a natural who can take what he wants and who can use others.

To his loyal, supportive wife, Linda, who makes do on his diminishing income—which he exaggerates when he reports it to her—and who pampers his hopes and soothes his ego, Willy is gruff and impatient. He is also disloyal to her and to their marriage. When Biff realizes, by discovering Willy's adultery, the fabric of lies of which their life is woven, he becomes broken and disenchanted, a vagrant and a failure. Only through a confrontation with his father in which his hatred and his love can explode into expression does he achieve the possibility of renewal and authentic existence.

For Willy, it is too late. He has betrayed his family *and* himself because he has been fashioned by social values and economic necessity. As a socially determined being, he has lived by the only rules he knows, but they are the rules of a world that is brutal in its economics and not supportive. Pursuing the appearance of commercial success, he has abandoned whatever of himself was authentic and self-fulfilling. His life culminates in envy and resentment; he is easily irritated and wanders into fantasy. When everything is going wrong for him—that is, once he is no longer useful—he virtually does not exist for the people he worked for, and he therefore loses the identity built on their regard. In fact, he has never existed if not as a commodity.

What the spectators see is that Willy exists only as an illusion of himself. His negation is Miller's indictment of the system (called sometimes capitalism, sometimes conformity, and sometimes the American Dream) that negated him. Conforming to the role and adhering to the value of being someone who must always be *selling* and is always *sold* finally kill him. In the world, as a commodity, he is worth more dead than alive.

In *The Crucible*, the village of Salem is swept up in hysteria over diabolical possession and witchcraft—hysteria generated dramatically, if not quite historically, by unfulfilled sexual desire—and the character John Proctor is caught in the maelstrom. He must betray himself and others, conforming to the demands of his society in order to live, or he must die to preserve truth, his name, and the good names of others. The paradox of attaining individual authenticity through negation of oneself as a member of society defines the nature of tragedy and of heroism in much of Miller's work. The forces ranged against us, both those coming as social forces from without and those constituted by the demonic forces of our own individual and racial psychology, may be inevitable and insurmountable. Yet that does not mean, according to the code Miller lays down in his plays, that we cannot oppose them. By the heroism of this resistance, moreover, we may reconstitute their nature and ours and may recover the possibilities of existence, even in death.

Miller's belief in the social determination of human action and in the power of social forces is mitigated by his belief in a moral responsibility that his characters are challenged to exercise through sacrifice and the awareness of otherness that Miller believes mankind is able to exercise:

> I had made no bones about being a rather impatient moralist, not even in interviews, where I was naïve enough to confess

that to me an immoral art was a contradiction and an artist was obliged to point a way out if he knew what it was. I had unknowingly picked up where my beloved Russians had left off, but without Tolstoy's and Dostoyevsky's privilege of a god whose unearthly resolutions, as in *Crime and Punishment*, one did not have to believe in reasonably but only sense to validate. I was striving toward a sensation of religious superreality that did not, however, depart the conditions of earth, a vision of avoidance of evil that would thrill even atheists and lead them "upward." ... The more exactingly true a character or dilemma was, the more spiritualized it became. (*Timebends*, 145)

In Miller's 1945 Broadway hit *All My Sons*, an industrialist profiteers during the war selling the army defective airplane engines and is thereby responsible for the death of American pilots; then he passes the blame to an associate, who is sent to prison in his place. Miller lodges the fault not within the social values, even though he makes it clear that they are corrupt, but within Joe Keller, the man who puts cupidity and self-interest above the good of others:

> KELLER: ... Who worked for nothin' in that war? When they work for nothin,' I'll work for nothin.' Did they ship a gun or a truck outa Detroit before they got their price? Is that clean? It's dollars and cents, nickels and dimes; war and peace, it's nickels and dimes, what's clean? Half the Goddam country is gotta go [to prison] if I go! ... Then ... why am I bad?
> CHRIS [his son]: *I* know you're no worse than most men but I thought you were better. (*Eight Plays*, 88)

In this play, the capitalism that Miller so often deplores is not only a systemic social force negatively influencing human behavior but also the result of a character disposition in each particular man. Joe Keller is not mistaken in his understanding of how things are done or in his indictment of others. He is at fault for his own similar behavior. Individual acts of greed and aggression become systemic and come to define a totality by the values and choices of many men. In Miller's work, the fact that we are capable of individually *choosing* evil demonstrates that we are able to make things better collectively by individually abjuring such a choice. Miller shares the traditional stance of those who see humanity endowed with a moral capability.

Miller's view of human psychology in play after play is constructed on the belief in the existence of a moral human capability as well as sociological determinism. What determines how things turn out and the conditions that surround us—in other words, what determines the determining systems as well as what they determine—are the values and actions people choose and the tension between the human ability to see clearly and the human tendency to blindness, to resist seeing. It is a ceaseless circle of causes and effects that are continuously transmuting into each other.

In Miller's understanding of human psychology, there are ontological forces independent of social causation. True, although they can just as soon be given form and direction by the social reality as give it direction, individual response to that reality matters. Individuals define themselves by their blindness or insight, and their blindness or insight affects the potency and effectiveness of these forces.

This is not very different from the idea of tragedy in the plays of Sophocles. Oedipus's blindness is inevitable and, therefore, is his fate, but his blindness is the source of the audience's insight, and the caution that he spurned, the audience, through his example, can learn to practice, as if he were a sacrifice. That is why a character like Oedipus is not only tragic but also a tragic *hero*. He undergoes what the spectators will not have to undergo if they pay attention to his story.

The machinery of tragedy is also what powers *A View from the Bridge* (1957), a melodrama whose passion reaches operatic intensity (in fact, the play was made into an opera in 2001 by William Bolcolm). In this play, longshoreman Eddie Carbone is jealously and murderously in love with his niece and betrays his name, his honor, and his bond with his community and the people who depend on him in pursuit of a blind love. As rooted as it is in the verisimilitude of the Red Hook culture of Brooklyn, *A View from the Bridge* is one of Miller's plays least concerned with social issues, analysis, or criticism and is most concerned with illuminating primal human forces.

Clara (1986), on the other hand, a play as reserved as *Bridge* is overwrought, attains its tragic status by showing the sacrifice a socially unjust system exacts of those who devote themselves to making justice prevail and who exercise (perhaps) willful blindness. In *Clara*, a man's daughter, an idealistic social worker, has been murdered (probably by one of the former prisoners whom she has counseled and with whom she had become a lover) because she lived according to and trusted in the (right, good, and humane) ideals her father taught her. Here, as he so often does, Miller has constructed a drama reflecting the conflict that arises because of the break in congruence between an inner vision and the reality of an external system. It is a particularly difficult task that he undertakes in *Clara* because he is testing the progressive values he espouses and is laying out their possible cost and the sacrifice they demand.

Fine is the policeman trying to solve the murder. Kroll, Clara's father, is being questioned by him as he tries to uncover information that will help him figure out who the killer might be:

> FINE: I figure we're both on the same side, right?
> KROLL: (after a pause) Excuse me saying it, but I would have thought, being Jewish, that you'd have been more understanding ... of this kind of situation. I mean, you're suddenly faced with an underprivileged man like that, you just naturally feel ...
> FINE: Yes, I know what you mean. I used to. I used to have a lot of understanding. But I gave up on it.
> KROLL: I see.
> FINE: I couldn't deny it. I finally had to face it—I have my limitations; Jewish or not Jewish, I think a man who cuts off a woman's head is a criminal. And if he's been discriminated against and had a bad upbringing, I can only tell you that most of the Puerto Rican people don't become criminals and they have the same background. I used to have a lot of questions about life, but in these last years I'm down to two—what did the guy do, and can I prove it? Whether his mother left him in the same shitty diaper for weeks at a time is not our problem. (*Danger: Memory!*, 53-54)

Because of the consequences of the hidden dangers that constitute reality and a frequent refusal to credit circumstances, as Fine refuses to do in *Clara*, Miller sees the playwright as one who must be "the destroyer of chaos, a man privy to the councils of the hidden gods who administer the hidden laws that bind us all and destroy us if we do not know them. And chaos, for one thing, was life lived oblivious of history." (Seibold, 54)

This is the Promethean moral project of his work. The writer, according to Miller, serves humanity by his penetration and representation of the actualities that constitute and surround us because of the ameliorative power of knowledge. In a 1965 essay, "Guilt and Incident at Vichy," Miller writes: "If the hostility and aggression which lie hidden in every human being could be accepted as a fact rather than as reprehensible sin, perhaps the race could begin to guard against its ravages." (*Echoes Down the Corridor*, 74)

II

Even though Miller's plays generally confront problems that arise because of the conflict between an imperfect individual and an unjust society and, except for *After the Fall*, do not seem autobiographical as does Eugene O'Neill's *Long Day's Journey into Night*, for example, and despite the universal appeal of many of his plays—*Death of a Salesman* having been translated into more than 50 languages and even produced in Beijing in Chinese—a great deal of the material of Miller's life has supplied the content of his plays. (Clurman, vii) The composition of Miller's family, for example, and their relationships to each other and to the period in which they lived and that shaped them, are of seminal importance to his dramaturgy, providing character templates and thematic nuggets from which his plays are generated. Miller himself suggests the archetypal dramatic paradigm his family was for him, conceived within the framework of a game of chess:

> Playfully my mind would set up chessboard arrangements, the pieces being father, mother, brother, sister, each with different powers and rights-of-way, imperious in one direction while vulnerable and paralyzed in another. Regardless of how the game played out, it had to end the same way, in a confrontation with the father after I had picked off sister and mother and pushed brother beyond reach of effective action. The father could move in all directions, and his decree of punishment, of course, was always death. (*Timebends*, 145)

At the onset of the Great Depression, Miller's own immigrant father lost everything, including his wife's esteem, his own sense of self-worth, and his son's undisturbed regard. Fallen, he served as the model for an archetypal figure in Miller's plays, the ambiguous father about whom a son can have only ambivalent feelings. In part, he was the model for Willy Loman in *Death of a Salesman*, Joe Keller in *All My Sons*, Quentin's father in *After the Fall*, the dead father in *The Price*, and Lee Baum's father in *The American Clock*. In these plays, the father is both loved and hated; he can take the form of a dedicated family man, a tyrant, a philanderer, a cheater, an exploiter, a failure, even a criminal; he is a man who does all he can to survive, caring and callous, a character simultaneously capable of both loyalty and treachery and who calls up these reactions to himself in others. For his sons, he is a shaping power that must be confronted.

Miller adored his mother, Augusta (Gussie), who seems to have been an unsteady mixture of generosity and recrimination. She was artistic in temperament, played the piano, went to the theater, and paid a student from Columbia University to come to her home and discuss literature with her. The Depression embittered her. She resented her husband for the loss of his business and his fortune. She also put the family, which in flush times had spent without counting, on a strict budget, played cards for money, and finagled credit.

She, too, is a model for a series of characters. Linda Loman is an idealized version, more supportive of Willy than Gussie was of Isadore Miller but, like her, shrewd in keeping a household going despite little money. She appears at her most unsympathetic as Quentin's mother in *After the Fall*; as Lee Baum's mother, Rose, in *The American Clock*; and as the remembered mother of Victor and Walter Franz in *The Price*—in each play berating the father for his failure in the Depression.

Variations on his chess fantasy of relegating the figure of his brother, Kermit, to a subsidiary and subordinate place, "beyond the reach of effective action," often appear in Miller's plays. So do versions of a fraternal relationship defined by a tension between bond and rivalry, showing the ambivalence of fraternal connection and alienation. *The Man Who Had All the Luck* (1944), even though a Broadway flop and hardly known among the plays in the Miller corpus, is an important play in Miller's formation as a playwright. He writes that this play, "through its endless versions, was to move me inch by inch toward my first open awareness of father–son and brother–brother conflict." (*Timebends*, 90) As he worked on it, characters who were initially conceived of as friends were made brothers, and the father of one became the father of both. Miller saw this development as charging the story with "a different anguish." (91)

In his next play, *All My Sons*, the sexual rival/older brother has died in the war. In *Death of a Salesman*, Happy Loman, the younger brother, is drawn as someone his mother can justly call "a philandering bum." (*Eight Plays*, 135) His story, unlike his brother Biff's, is hardly the concern of the drama. In *The Creation of the World* (1972), the primal fratricide, Cain's slaughter of Abel, is represented. In *The Price* (1968), the complex relationship of fraternity and fratricide makes up the entire matter of the play. Victor believes that in his youth, years before the play begins, he had sacrificed his future to care for his father and that his brother, Walter, callously turned his back on them both in order to pursue success:

> WALTER: And if I said—Victor, if I said that I did have some wish to hold you back? What would that give you now?
> VICTOR: Is that what you wanted? ...
> WALTER: I wanted the freedom to do my work. Does that mean I stole your life? ... And you? You never had any hatred for me? Never a wish to see me destroyed? To destroy me, to destroy me with this saintly self-sacrifice, this mockery of sacrifice? (*Eight Plays*, 716)

In fact, there is something resembling the division between Walter and Victor in the roles Arthur and Kermit Miller played in relation to their father. In his autobiography, *Timebends: A Life*, Arthur writes, "I wanted and did not want to excel over my brother." (*Timebends*, 276) His brother "had to drop out of NYU [New York University] to assist my father in another of his soon-to-fail coat businesses," and "was ... busy mobilizing himself to save our father, whom he had romanticized into a fallen giant." (108, 116) Arthur "felt some guilt [like Walter in *The Price*] for having left him to prop up the family while I, the inferior student, went off to college" (226) and that his brother, like Victor in *The Price*, "was in service to the idealized father just as I [Miller himself] was enlisted in that ideal's destruction." (226)

In plays like *After the Fall* and *The Archbishop's Ceiling*, fraternal consanguinity is replaced by the social and professional ideas of brotherhood. The bond in *After the Fall* between Mickey and Quentin, which is based on Miller's friendship with Elia Kazan, is like a bond between brothers who, despite their regard and their love for each other, are torn apart by their conflicting values and mutually excluding choices.

In *The Archbishop's Ceiling*, the suspiciousness resulting from the spying and bugging practiced by an Eastern European Communist regime modeled on Czechoslovakia serves to erode the bond of brotherhood, play into professional jealousy, and undermine creative cross-fertilization between writers.

> SIGMUND: When I was young writer, Marcus was the most famous novelist in our country. In Stalin time he was six years in prison. He cannot write. I was not in prison. When he has returned I am very popular, but he was forgotten. It is tragic story.
> ADRIAN: You mean he's envious of you.
> SIGMUND: This is natural. (*The Archbishop's Ceiling*, 51)

Miller first introduces the family unit that will dominate the *dramatis personae* of his work in his 1935 unpublished play, variously called *No Villain*, *They Too Arise*, and *The Grass Still Grows*. In conformance with his own family, there are two brothers and a sister, but she is dropped from the play early in its development and does not reappear in any of the nuclear families at the core of his later work either.

In 1929, 14-year-old Arthur left upper Manhattan and the ease that had kept him oblivious to economic suffering but that his father's inclusion in the Depression alerted him to; the Miller family moved to a small house in Brooklyn. Arthur dedicated most of his energy in high school to athletics rather than scholarship and failed to be accepted by the University of Michigan when he was graduated in 1932. However, he formed his understanding of life on the street. He saw people lined up in front of banks when the doors were locked. The bicycle he had bought with money he had withdrawn the day before the banks were shut down was stolen two days later. He was disoriented and ashamed when his father changed from a determined, forceful provider, proud of his accomplishments and power, into a chastened man guilty over his loss and humiliated by his incapacity to earn a living. He saw his mother become waspish with disappointment. This aspect of his mother recurs throughout his work, in *After the Fall*, *The Price*, and *The American Clock*. *Clock* also dramatizes the bicycle incident and his father's transformation.

Miller's job in an auto parts warehouse in New York City served as the basis for his 1957 one-act play *A Memory of Two Mondays*. He drove a truck around the garment district and was illuminated by a friend outside the neighborhood drugstore who explained Marxian economics, the Depression, the inevitable failure of capitalism and the socialist future to him between rounds of a handball game. That explanation relieved him of his burden of shame for his father. "If Marxism was, on the metaphorical plane, a rationale for parricide," he writes in *Timebends*, his 1986 autobiography, "I think that to me it was at the same time a way of forgiving my father, for it showed him as a kind of digit in a nearly cosmic catastrophe that was beyond his power to avoid."

Tellingly, for the moral philosophical outlook that informs his plays, which mixes determinism and responsibility, Miller adds two interesting points. The first is that his father would have to concede "that it was not his fault that he had failed." This insight, according to Miller, is the engine that would allow that failure to become the first step in a struggle against the system that had defeated him. Characteristic of Miler's world view, it shows the importance of awareness: failure itself is not a fault, but failure to realize that it is not, *is*; *that* is a failure to become class-conscious and thereby capable of changing society's circumstances. The second point suggests the complementary psychological foundation of Miller's concepts of people in society: his assertion that "the Depression was as much an occasion as a cause of such father-son collisions" as his with his father.

To the young Miller, "the Depression was only incidentally a matter of money.... it was a moral catastrophe, a violent revelation of the hypocrisies behind the façade of American society." (*The Archbishop's Ceiling*, 115)

Thus, he came to share with many people of that time hopeful faith in what appeared to be a try at social and economic justice in the Soviet Union. Nevertheless, he didn't become so dazzled as to pledge his loyalty to the Soviet image so deeply as to be thrown off balance or feel the need to defend himself against being compromised when the mendacity and brutality of Stalinism became clear. Nor did he need the strength of Soviet authority to maintain his critical vision of America throughout his life. In 1934, having saved money and having begun to read literature on his own, particularly Tolstoy and Dostoevsky, he was admitted to the University of Michigan on the strength of a letter he wrote to the dean asking for a chance to prove himself. (*Echoes*, 14)

At the university, he began writing plays and won several prizes. In 1936 he won the Avery Hopwood Award in Drama for *Honors at Dawn* and, in 1937, the Hopwood Award in Drama for *No Villain*, "the story of a strike in a garment factory that set a son against his proprietor father," and in which he used "members of my family for models." (*Echoes*, 91) In 1938, the year of his graduation, he received the $1,250 Theatre Guild National Award.

Miller also wrote for the *Michigan Daily* and covered the strike at the General Motors Fisher Body Plant in Flint. He interviewed strike leader Walter Reuther, later head of the United Auto Workers. Miller writes that he sensed "a new beauty was being born" and felt enthusiasm for unionism which, he adds, a decade later he found tempered by the development in some unions of "a new power to coerce ... one that would often turn a cynical gangster face to the world." It was, in fact, pressure from the longshoreman's union a little more than a decade later that persuaded Harry Cohn, the head of Columbia Pictures, not to shoot a movie script Miller had written about the brutality and crimes of Brooklyn waterfront union big shots. (*Echoes*, 267)

Such was his success as a playwright in college that Miller was offered a job writing screenplays in Hollywood for Twentieth Century-Fox pictures after graduation. He returned, however, to New York City to work for much less money as a playwright with the Federal Theatre Project, wishing to write for the working class in a working-class milieu. The condition of being told what to write and not having full control over how his writing would be used or changed was intolerable to him, whether it was the result of a discipline imposed by Hollywood, Moscow, or the House Un-American Activities Committee (HUAC). (*Echoes*, 411)

In 1940, Miller married Mary Grace Slattery and became a journeyman writer for CBS radio, creating *Cavalcade of America* scripts, dramatic vignettes celebrating American History. A football injury kept him out of the army in World War II, but he toured army bases to gather material for a movie script he had agreed to write, *The Story of G. I. Joe*. He withdrew from that project when his script was changed, but he used his research as the basis for a book called *Situation Normal*, about the dedication of soldiers in World War II to each other and to their common belief in the ideals for which they fought. Miller predicted that they would experience disorientation and alienation on returning to the comparative emptiness and purposelessness of civilian routines. (*Echoes*, 32–33)

After the failure of *The Man Who Had All the Luck* and before embarking on *All My Sons*, Miller wrote *Focus* (1945), a novel about anti-Semitism. In it he introduced several of his seminal themes. Besides the problem of violence against Jews, the novel presents the hero's discovery of the courage within to resist, even at great cost, the force of an external evil that demands capitulation. It is a theme that, along with its opposite, courage's failure, lies at the heart of *All My Sons*, *The Crucible*, *The Misfits* (1961), *Incident at Vichy* (1965), *Playing for Time* (1980), and *The Archbishop's Ceiling* (1984). It is also a theme that sounded in Miller's life.

The second great formative social event for Miller after the Depression was the escalation of McCarthyism, which began with the inception of the Cold War at the end of the 1940s, and flourished in the 1950s. Just as the Depression had robbed his family of its wealth and comfortable identity but had brought him an awareness of socioeconomic foundations and a sense of class consciousness and social justice, McCarthyism threatened the esteem and mobility that the success and celebrity of becoming a Pulitzer Prize–winning playwright (for *Death of a Salesman*) had brought him as well as having provided him the opportunity to define himself and to practice the courage to be authentic.

Miller was called to testify before the HUAC about his past beliefs and associations. What Communist activities had he participated in? Whom could he identify as having been a Communist or fellow traveler? He was forthcoming about his own ideas and beliefs; he acknowledged having attended meetings with Communist writers but refused to give the Committee names. He was held in contempt, fined $500, and given a year's suspended sentence. In 1958 the U.S. Court of Appeals for the District of Columbia overturned the judgment.

His friend and the director of both *All My Sons* and *Death of A Salesman*, Elia Kazan, already had given names to the Committee willingly and with a sense of doing right. No less than Kazan, Miller accepted the truth of the revelations of the corruption of Communism in the Soviet Union and that under Stalinism it was a deadly, antidemocratic system of brutality and betrayal. Miller also knew that some American Communists had compromised their integrity by overlooking or lying about Soviet barbarities they actually knew of.

To Kazan, these things justified cooperating with the HUAC. (*Eight Plays*, 504-506) Miller, however, saw the investigations themselves as doing violence to democracy by limiting the freedoms of thought, speech, hope, and imagination to ideologically acceptable formulas, thus recapitulating in American terms a Soviet evil. Perhaps even more significantly, he saw the hearings as undermining individual integrity and its foundation, our struggle to shape our own consciousness, to participate in shaping the world, and our obligation to value the integrity of others. In *All My Sons*, Chris Keller says to his father, "there's a universe of people outside, and you're responsible to it." (*Eight Plays*, 90)

The Crucible (1952), essentially an allegory, uses the 1692 Salem witchcraft trials to symbolize the 1950s anti-Communist purges. The play speaks to the condition of many who were summoned by the HUAC and foreshadows Miller's situation vis-à-vis the Committee and his response to it. In *The Crucible*, in order to save himself from hanging, John Proctor agrees to confess that he has had dealings with the Devil; however, that is not enough. He is required to name others whom he saw conspiring with the devil (just as witnesses called to testify before the HUAC were required to name people they saw at meetings or believed to be Communists), and he refuses to cooperate. When the chief judge/inquisitor demands of Proctor why, he cries out: "I have three children—how may I teach them to walk like men in the world, and I sold my friends?" (*Eight Plays*, 331)

Miller's ethic is founded on the belief that to betray others involves a betrayal of oneself. It entails a violation of and a loss of one's own name. The precious value of one's own name is asserted by John Proctor as well as by Willy Loman and Eddie Carbone, who in *A View from the Bridge* has informed on others, and it predates Miller's encounter with the Committee or even its dramatic presentation in *The Crucible*. The attack upon the lie that hides true identity is a recurring pattern in Miller's plays. It is at the crux of the drama of *All My Sons*, *Death of A Salesman*, his adaptation of Ibsen's *Enemy of the People*, and many of the plays written after the demise of McCarthyism.

In *Death of a Salesman*, Willy Loman's son Biff climactically and triumphantly asserts the truth of who he is against the grandiose illusions Willy has pressed him to live by and believe:

BIFF: Pop! I'm a dime a dozen, and so are you!
WILLY: I am not a dime a dozen! I am Willy Loman, and you are Biff Loman!
BIFF: I am not a leader of men, Willy, and neither are you. You were never anything but a hard-working drummer who landed in the ash can like all the rest of them! I'm one dollar an hour, Willy! I tried seven states and couldn't raise it. A buck an hour! Do you gather my meaning? I'm not bringing home any prizes any more, and you're going to stop waiting for me to bring them home! (*Eight Plays*, 201)

In *A View from the Bridge*, Eddie Carbone, in his dying fight with Marco, after Marco has rightly called him a liar, cries, "I want my good name, Marco. You took my name." (*A View From the Bridge*, 159)

Although Miller and Kazan broke with each other over giving names to the HUAC, in 1964 they worked together again at the inauguration of the ill-starred Lincoln Center Repertory Theater. Kazan directed *After the Fall*, Miller's most overtly autobiographical play and the one that includes his dramatization of and reflections on the conflicts of characters based on himself, Kazan, and several others who were subpoenaed to testify about their past Communist affiliations and associates.

Miller withstood that ordeal, just as he had survived the Depression and World War II, and like every Jew living after World War II, even Jews who were not in Europe but safe in the United States, he survived the Holocaust. Both survival and success are significant themes in his plays, microcosmically with regard to his father and brother and macrocosmically with regard to the political and racial brutality of the 20th century. One of the challenges Miller confronted in his plays and in his life was to understand and cope with the guilt that, for him, must accompany survival and success because so many other people, through social conditions and no fault of their own, are brought to failure or even death.

The Man Who Had All the Luck, Miller's first Broadway play, is charged, he has written, with an "obsessive terror of failure and ... guilt for success," which "was reinforced by leftist egalitarian convictions."

(*Timebends*, 139) Following the success of *All My Sons*, which "was bringing in some two thousand a week," (276) Miller writes that

> [a]fter some weeks, realizing as I sat down to dinner with Mary in our Brooklyn Heights house that the Coronet Theater was about to fill up yet again that evening with paying customers and that my words had a power beyond my mere self, I felt a certain threat along with the inevitable exhilaration.... My identification with life's failures was being menaced by my fame, and this led me, a few weeks after the opening of *All My Sons*, to apply at the New York State Employment Service for any job available. I was sent out to a factory in Long Island City to stand all day assembling beer box dividers for the minimum wage. The grinding boredom and the unnaturalness of my pretense to anonymity soon drove me out of the place, but the question remained as to how to live without breaking contact with ... the ones in the audience who made the pants and filled the teeth. It was not merely a question of continuing to draw material from life but also a moral one. (*Timebends*, 138-39)

Miller's guilt at success can also be understood as resulting from his ambivalent feelings of esteem and contempt for his father, Isadore, from whom he learned the ways of success until age 14, when he began to learn the ways of failure from him. Freud's discovery at the end of his 1937 essay "A Disturbance of Memory on the Acropolis," fits Miller's situation equally well: "It seems as if the essence of success were to have got further than one's father, and as though to excel one's father were still something forbidden." (Freud, 320)

In *The Price* (1968), the difference in their relation to their father provides the conflict between Victor, the police sergeant, who is a failure in his own and in his wife's eyes, and his brother Walter, the successful surgeon, and it shapes their inner conflicts as well. At the root of that conflict is the contradiction in their responses to their father's failure when he lost his fortune because of the crash and Victor surrendered his hopes in order to care for him while Walter followed his own ambition. The primal fratricide also turns on the issue of failure and success in *The Creation of the World and Other Business* (1972) when Abel's sacrifice delights God and Cain's offering fails to.

Even more than having survived the Depression or the anti-Communist witch-hunts or the possibility of failing or succeeding as a person, a writer, or a husband, surviving the Holocaust, according to Miller, is a chief reason for guilt. In *Timebends*, his autobiography, Miller writes not only of his own feelings but also of the experience of his third wife, the photographer Inge (Ingeborg) Morath (who died in February 2002). Born in Austria, although she was not Jewish, when she refused to join the Nazis, she was made to assemble airplane parts in a German war factory as a slave laborer. In *After the Fall*, the character of Holga, based on her, says, "no one is innocent they did not kill." (*Eight Plays*, 561) It is a theme Miller takes up in *Playing for Time* (1980), a television screenplay based on Fania Fenelon's diaries of her life as a prisoner in a Nazi death camp:

> *Cut to the dayroom. Evening. Mengele, Kramer, and Mandel listen to the orchestra, ... Fania, accompanying herself, is singing "Un Bel Di" in an agonized and therefore extraordinarily moving way. When she [finishes] Mandel stands, applauding—he is excited as a patron, a discoverer of talent....*
> MANDEL: Did you ever hear anything more touching, Herr Commandant?
> KRAMER: Fantastic. *To Mengele*: But Dr. Mengele's musical opinions are more expert, of course.
> *Cut to Fania, staring at the ultimate horror—their love for her music ...*
> MENGELE: I have rarely felt so totally—moved.
> *And he appears, in fact to have been deeply stirred* (*Plays: Two*, 481)

That the Holocaust has psychological effects figures, too, in the psychodynamics of *Broken Glass* (1994), a complex family drama set in November 1938 about sexual frustration; hysterical paralysis; Nazi persecution of Jews, especially during *Kristallnacht* (the night of broken glass); and the psychological effect of that persecution on people as far away from Germany as Brooklyn.

The ambiguities of success and failure and the guilt of the survivor comprise the dramatic and philosophical core of *Incident at Vichy* (1965), a play set inside Gestapo headquarters in "unoccupied" France. Among those rounded up by the Nazis for a routine identity papers check are a Jewish psychiatrist, obviously slated for death, and a nobleman, Von Berg, a German aristocrat of the old school whose character is marked by grace, refinement, and *noblesse oblige*. It is obvious to him and to Leduc, the psychiatrist, that Von Berg will be given a pass and allowed to leave and that Leduc is among those to be incinerated.

The drama at the core of the play involves Von Berg's substituting himself as the victim for Leduc. Such self-abnegation, as in *The Crucible*, is, for Miller, essential self-assertion. It confirms the humanity the Nazis deny and asserts the possibility of action when justice seems to be impossible. "It's not your guilt I want," Leduc tells Von Berg near the end of *Vichy*, "it's your responsibility." (*Eight Plays*, 627)

Miller the moralist presents the spectators with a discomforting moral imperative: guilt must be transformed into responsibility, and that requires sacrifice. The definition of responsibility to emerge from Miller's plays joins duty to oneself, duty to others, and duty to overriding values into a unity. What happens to others and what happens to ourselves are inextricably plaited and have the same origins. In *Broken Glass*, Sylvia Gellburg is paralyzed in Brooklyn because of the atrocities Germans are enacting against Jews in Berlin and because of the circumstances of her marital life.

Part of Miller's own struggle with himself as he became successful involved his ability to maintain his authenticity as a writer and not to lose himself to success by becoming a false image of himself. Writing about the effects of the success of *Death of a Salesman* on him in 1949, he observed:

> I had striven all my life to win this night, and it was here, and I was this celebrated man who had amazingly little to do with me, or I with him.... fame is the other side of loneliness, of impossible-to-resolve contradictions—to be anonymous and at the same time not lose one's renown, in brief, to be two people who might occasionally visit together and perhaps make a necessary joint public appearance but who would normally live separate lives, the public fellow wasting his time gadding about while the writer stayed at his desk, as morose and anxious as ever, and at work. I did not want the power I wanted. It wasn't "real." What was? (*Timebends*, 194)

One way in which Miller shielded himself from the guilt of success—besides wryly noting that, for Communists in a capitalist society, success was an indication of failure—was by using what power of renown or celebrity was his to exercise a responsibility not only literary. He continued to be as politically engaged as he had been before his success and before being subpoenaed by the HUAC, although he was for a time stripped of his passport and was also prevented from following through on several projects, including a screenplay about juvenile delinquency that he had researched in the streets of Brooklyn.

He was active in the movement to stop the war in Vietnam and was a peace delegate at the bloody Chicago convention of the Democratic Party in 1968. His protests against Soviet anti-Semitism and Soviet censorship of writers led to the shutting down of a production of *Incident at Vichy* in Moscow.

His concerns were both worldwide and local. In 1965 he became the president of the International PEN Club (Poets, Essayists, and Novelists), an organization designed to foster dialogue among writers from differing cultures, to promote world peace, and to protect writers censored or persecuted for their work and their beliefs. PEN, at the time he assumed its presidency, was moribund, and Miller brought it back to life with the prestige of his name; the scope of his contacts, especially in Soviet-dominated Eastern Europe and the Soviet Union itself; and his even-handed opposition to all censorship and any ideological cant. His experiences visiting Prague as president of PEN; meeting playwright Václav Havel (later to be president of Czechoslovakia, after the Soviet occupation ended); and seeing what it was like always to be aware that private conversations were being overheard by the authorities through secretly planted listening devices, served as the basis for *The Archbishop's Ceiling*.

In 1973, he became active in defense of Peter Reilly, an 18-year-old Connecticut boy wrongly convicted of murdering his mother and ultimately helped overturn his conviction and free him from lifelong imprisonment. During the effort to impeach President Clinton, he wrote an op-ed piece in *The New York Times* disparaging what he saw as a culture of self-righteous Puritanism.

III

Playwriting itself, however, was Miller's primary form of activism. "I could not," he has written, "imagine a theater worth my time that did not want to change the world"; however, "to do that it had to reach precisely those who accepted everything as it was." (*Timebends*, 180) Therefore theater could not be, for Miller's purposes, the avant-garde or absurd or experimental enterprise it was among some European intellectuals and disaffected Americans. It had to be a theater with a popular base, striving to find a "big audience," the commercial theater of Broadway.

For Miller, then, from the start of his career, "the playwright's challenge was to please not a small sensitized supporting clique but an audience representing, more or less, all America." (*Timebends*, 179) He imagined himself not as solitary and isolated, as an intellectual or an artist working hermetically, catering to a specialized audience, but as a popular writer for a commercial theater. The characters and situations he created emerge from the realities of common experience, not fantastically from the writer's imagination or his metaphysics.

It has been Miller's gift to be able to express in many of his plays the spirit of a time, the experiences of a people, and the complexity of their characters and motivations in specific and concrete dramatic situations. Miller is an American playwright embodying the multiplicity of interests, classes, styles, desires, and points of view that coexist, not without tension and sometimes with hostility, to make American culture. It is a culture of contradictions, and Miller himself, in his work and in his life, embodies those contradictions. He is the New York, working class, Jewish intellectual who comprehends social injustice and wants to change the world and simultaneously an international celebrity with wealth, mobility, and connections and at one time even the husband of Marilyn Monroe, for whom he wrote the screenplay of the 1961 film *The Misfits*, directed by John Huston.

Indeed, his ambition for a career as a playwright embraced a contradiction. Reflecting on the American theater in the 1940s, Miller writes, "I thought the theater a temple being rotted out with commercialized junk." Immediately correcting himself, however, he adds, "it was also a time when the audience was basically the same for musicals and light entertainment as for the ambitious stuff and had not yet been atomized ... into the young and old, hip and square, or even political left and middle and right." (*Timebends*, 179)

The challenge for Miller in the 1940s, therefore, was to write plays that affected a broad range of people by looking familiar and yet going beyond the familiar. His work had to penetrate surface conventions and beliefs, confront problems and deal with issues which, left undisturbed, permitted the social order and the economic system to continue unexamined and unthreatened. The way he went about it was by making plays that on the surface looked familiar, like other Broadway plays. Indeed, Miller's plays look more like the plays of such providers of light fare for the American theater as Philip Barry or Kaufman and Hart than like the radical additions to world dramatic literature by Bertolt Brecht or Luigi Pirandello. For the content and style of his plays, however, Miller drew upon the material, emotional, and spiritual conflicts that arise in unjust and usually capitalist societies when individuals confront each other and their circumstances. Miller is like a serious composer in the 20th century who composes harmonic and melodic music despite the esteem it has surrendered to a highly fashionable but limitedly appealing atonality. His choice, reminiscent of one Aaron Copland made early in his career, was to reach a large and popular audience without yielding his integrity or pandering.

Despite their social and moral agenda, Miller's plays are not ideological tracts but compelling art, primarily because of the breadth of his sympathy for his characters and for the diversity of responses that can be encompassed within humanity. Miller appended an "Author's Production Note" to *The Price*, which, in this regard, is instructive beyond its advice to the players:

> A fine balance of sympathy should be maintained in the playing of the roles of Victor and Walter.... The admonition goes beyond the question of theatrics to the theme of the play. As the world now operates, the qualities of both brothers are necessary to it; surely their respective psychologies and moral values conflict at the heart of the social dilemma. The production must therefore withhold judgement in favor of presenting both men in all their humanity and from their own viewpoints. (*Eight Plays*, 721)

Rather than demonize particular points of view, Miller strives to dramatize the humanity in them. He does so by generating powerful emotional responses in his audiences. Although they are dramas of ideas and choices, his plays are not cerebral and do not cultivate the distancing devices of alienation. The plays involve the audience.

A survey of Miller's plays, beginning with his first success in 1947, *All My Sons*, reveals the way in which Miller fused style and technique with the subject and the setting of the play. *All My Sons* is pure Ibsen, a well-plotted domestic drama through which spectators may seem to spy on a segment of life. Hidden in the drama and the lives of the characters is a concealed transgression, or a set of secret transgressions, whose revelation shatters an established order and makes plain inescapable illuminations and inevitable consequences. It is theater of passionate speeches: arguments, confessions, accusations, justifications, all leading toward a catastrophic revelation that restores the moral order through tragic action and loss, thus chastening the spectators and sharpening their perception regarding morality, integrity, and responsibility. Its aesthetics are those of an art whose purpose is moral education and the awful immediacy of the biblical prophets.

In *Death of a Salesman*, Miller takes the same dramatic kernel, the cluster of father, mother, and two sons—Willy Loman, with a secret guilt; Linda, his loyal wife; Biff, who vacillates between revering and despising his father; and Happy, the younger son whose greatest commitment is to his appetites—and moves it from the wealthy comfort of the suburbs to lower-middle-class Brooklyn and transforms the force that brings the father down from his own lack of concern for others to the capitalism that turns people into exploiters and the exploited. Rather than write a drama that illuminates the interior reality of character by exterior action and dialogue, Miller attempts to dramatize the psychological disintegration of his main character by allowing the spectators to cross the boundary between the world of outer reality and Willy Loman's interior existence with its memories, delusions, and hallucinations. The stagecraft allows the audience both to see Willy and to see what Willy sees. Miller's stage directions at the beginning of the play make it clear that he is bringing an expressionistic stagecraft into what is still an Ibsenian drama:

> The entire setting is wholly or, in some places, partially
> transparent. The roof line of the house is one-dimensional;

under and over it we see the apartment buildings. Before the house lies an apron, curving beyond the forestage into the orchestra. This forward area serves as the back yard as well as the locale of all Willy's imaginings and of his city scenes. Whenever the action is in the present the actors observe the imaginary wall lines, entering the house only through its door at the left. But in the scenes of the past these boundaries are broken, and characters enter or leave a room by stepping "through" a wall onto the forestage. (*Eight Plays*, 95)

Originally, a propos of these directions, Miller intended to call the play *Inside His Head*, a phenomenological title describing the construction of the play rather than a thematic title. Miller reverted to and extended the dramaturgy of *Death of a Salesman* in *After the Fall* (1964), the play that ushered in his middle period and, fittingly for its style, is his most obviously autobiographical.

"The action," as the first words of the stage directions inform us, "takes place in the mind, thought and memory of Quentin." (*Eight Plays*, 475) The set is appropriately fluid, making a stage not for spectacle or observation but for vision and rumination. The play seems designed less to show the arc of action than the recollection of events, less to express thought and feeling than to make oneself able to continue thinking and feeling after those fundamental processes have become apparently futile and palpably painful. There is no furniture except one chair, and there are "no walls or substantial boundaries." There are several curved platforms on several levels and "abutments, ledges, or crevices" which the actors use for seats when necessary.

Rising above the playing area "is the blasted stone tower of a German concentration camp." It has windows like eyes looking out at the scene, and "bent reinforcing rods stick out of it like broken tentacles." Existing as both a real historical instrument of inhumanity and a metaphor for inhumanity, it is the specter that informs and symbolizes all the other events of the protagonist's experience. The actors throughout the play "appear and disappear instantaneously, as in the mind, but it is not necessary that they walk off the stage." The stage is designed to give the impression of consciousness perceiving itself perceiving.

The play is constructed of narrative episodes, dramatic encounters, recurring memories and returning images, temporal and thematic conflations, and the protagonist's agonized reflections. Unlike most of Miller's plays, it fragments linear narrative and dramatic actions. They are shown as random mental threads, hauntings rather than meanings.

After the Fall presents the struggle to forge a unified consciousness and a hope on which to build a future life when the events of life in the macrocosm of the political world and the microcosm of the domestic one repeatedly show our failure of responsibility to one another and the failure or insufficiency of our love for each other.

Again, in the 1986 one-act play *Clara*, Miller uses expressionistic technique, but more as he did in *Death of a Salesman*. Since *Clara* is a play about discovering a repressed memory, it allows the spectators to move from the Ibsenian representation of a conversation between Clara's father and the policeman investigating her murder to the father's internal flashes of insight and episodes of memory. In *The American Clock*, too, Miller plays with disjunctive elements, narrative, memory, dramatic episodes, choral commentary, singing, and vaudeville hoofing. The *USA* trilogy by Dos Passos seems more to be its model than the theater of Thornton Wilder, appropriate enough for a work based on Studs Terkel's *Hard Times*, which offers multiple renditions of life during the Great Depression from a left-populist perspective.

As if recoiling from the sprawling mindscape of *After the Fall* and from the drubbing critics gave the play, the play that followed it, *Incident at Vichy*, is a sharply defined, tightly constructed piece, unambiguously set in the waiting area of Gestapo headquarters. Succeeding plays like *The Price*, *The Archbishop's Ceiling*, *I Can't Remember Anything*, *The Last Yankee*, *The Ride Down Mount Morgan*, and *Broken Glass* all share the traditional stagecraft of an Ibsen, Shaw, or Chekhov play. So do *The Crucible* and, for the most part, *A View from the Bridge*. In *The Creation of the World*, Miller deviates somewhat from this model, mixing the concrete, the ethereal, and the philosophical in a manner resembling Shaw's *Don Juan in Hell* sequence in *Man and Superman*.

What distinguishes *A View from the Bridge*, especially in its one-act version, is that it is written in verse, and in a perfectly natural way the actors move from dialogue into individual arias, stichometric sentences, and ensemble pieces. Both versions, the original and an expanded two-act version, use the lawyer Alfieri as a choral figure who speaks to the spectators; introduces the play; comments on the action; and, when necessary, assumes a role in the drama. The narrative frame, however, is there not to distance the spectators from the play but to give the play the immediacy of primary myth, a force so threatening that it needs the containment of a frame. This is what the lawyer Alfieri is suggesting in the epilogue:

> Most of the time now we settle for half
> And I like it better.
> And yet, when the tide is right
> And the green smell of the sea
> Floats in through my window,
> The waves of this bay
> Are the waves against Siracusa,
> And I see a face that suddenly seems carved;
> The eyes look like tunnels
> Leading back toward some ancestral beach
> Where all of us once lived.
> And I wonder at those times
> How much of us
> Really lives there yet,
> And when we will truly have moved on,
> On and away from that dark place,
> That world that has fallen to stones?
> (*A View From the Bridge*, 159-60)

This is not the sort of thing we expect from Miller, but here it is, relatively early in his work. Yet it indicates one of Miller's pervasive strategies: to imbue contemporary material with the monumental solidity of timeless reference even while dissecting the present causes and exposing the primarily social roots of present evils. Alfieri is not offering social analysis; he is referring to a primal wild nature that we share and that must affect our social action and help shape our principles but also that can be brutalized or utilized by the laws of our social institutions. Social constructs may or may not be responsible for the configuration of Eddie Carbone's character, but only they have devised the category illegal immigrant and have thereby facilitated Eddie's revenge by state power. It is the primal nature of which Alfieri speaks that has an undomesticated timelessness and reveals our presocially defined selves that Miller is showing in *A View from the Bridge*. It is what is lost by the mediation of social conventions to which we must adapt.

In the second version of *A View from the Bridge*, Alfieri concedes grudgingly, "... now we are quite civilized, quite American. Now we settle for half, and I like it better. I no longer keep a pistol in my filing cabinet." (*Eight Plays*, 398) Alfieri focuses precisely on the compromise that constitutes the dilemma at the heart of the dramatic conflict, and which has engaged Miller throughout his career—the conflict between self-embedded, self-generating desire and social awareness of people's social responsibility toward one another.

Thus, on the one hand, there is the primal mankind referred to by Alfieri, but it is dangerous and vulnerable, as in the examples of Eddie Carbone and Joe Keller in *All My Sons*, who did not act with regard to the fact that "there's a universe of people outside and you're responsible to it." On the other hand, there is the civilized way of living by halves, expressing half, accepting half, thinking of life as a thing and becoming a thing oneself, losing a sense that life is sacred, losing the authentic identity that Miller signifies so often in his plays with the words "my name." It is this sense of the sacred that Miller believes gives meaning to existence, for it is only in relation to the things we hold sacred that our real, rather than our socially perverted, self reveals itself. (*Timebends*, 438)

Works Cited

Clurman, Harold. "Biographical Notes." In *The Portable Arthur Miller*, edited by Christopher Bigsby. New York: Penguin Books, 1995.

Freud, Sigmund. "A Disturbance of Memory on the Acropolis." In *Character and Culture*, edited by Philip Rieff. New York: Collier Books, 1963.

Miller, Arthur. *Echoes Down the Corridor*, edited by Steven R. Centola. New York: Viking, 2000.

———. *The Archbishop's Ceiling; and The American Clock: Two Plays*. New York: Grove Press, 1989.

———. *Timebends: A Life*. New York: Grove Press, 1987.

———. *Danger: Memory!*, New York: Grove Press, 1986.

———. *Arthur Miller: Eight Plays.* Garden City, NY: Nelson Doubleday, Inc., 1981.

———. *Plays: Two.* London, 1981.

———. *A View from the Bridge: Two One-Act Plays by Arthur Miller.* New York: The Viking Press, 1965.

Seibold, Thomas, ed. *Readings on Arthur Miller.* San Diego: Greenhaven Press, 1997.

ORM ÖVERLAND

The Action and Its Significance:
Arthur Miller's Struggle with Dramatic Form

"There are two questions I ask myself over and over when I'm working," Arthur Miller has remarked. "What do I mean? What am I trying to say?"[1] The questions do not cease when a play is completed but continue to trouble him. In the "Introduction" to his *Collected Plays* Miller is constantly asking of each play: "What did I mean? What was I trying to say?" These questions and the playwright's attempts to answer them are directly related to his account of how he planned and wrote his next play.

The process of playwriting is given a peculiar wavelike rhythm in Miller's own story of his efforts to realize his intentions from one play to the other. Troughs of dejection on being exposed to unexpected critical and audience responses to a newly completed play are followed by swells of creativity informed by the dramatist's determination to make himself more clearly understood in the next one.[2] This wavelike rhythm of challenge and response is the underlying structural principle of Miller's "Introduction" to his *Collected Plays*. Behind it one may suspect the workings of a radical distrust of his chosen medium. The present essay will consider some of the effects both of this distrust of the theater as a means of communication and of Miller's theories of dramatic form on his career as a dramatist.

Arthur Miller is not alone in asking what he is trying to say in his plays, nor in being concerned that they may evoke other responses than

From *Modern Drama*, vol. XVIII, no .1 (March 1975). © 1975 by the University of Toronto, Graduate Centre for Study of Drama. Reprinted by permission.

those the playwright thought he had aimed at. From the early reviews of
Death of a Salesman critics have observed that a central problem in the
evaluation of Miller's work is a conflict of themes, real or apparent,
within each play.

The case for the prosecution has been well put by Eric Bentley:

> Mr. Miller says he is attempting a synthesis of the social and
> the psychological, and, though one may not see any
> synthesis, one certainly sees the thesis and the antithesis. In
> fact, one never knows what a Miller play is about: politics or
> sex. If *Death of a Salesman* is political, the key scene is the one
> with the tape recorder; if it's sexual, the key scene is the one
> in the Boston hotel. You may say of *The Crucible* that it isn't
> about McCarthy, it's about love in the seventeenth century.
> And you may say of *A View from the Bridge* that it isn't about
> informing, it's about incest and homosexuality.[3]

John Mander points to the same conflict in his analysis of *Death of a
Salesman* in his *The Writer and Commitment*:

> If we take the "psychological" motivation as primary, the
> "social" documentation seems gratuitous, if we take the
> "social" documentation as primary, the "psychological"
> motivation seems gratuitous. And we have, I am convinced,
> to choose which kind of motivation must have the priority;
> we cannot have both at once.[4]

Mr. Mander's own image of this conflict of themes within Arthur Miller's
play is the house divided and its two incompatible masters are Freud and
Marx.

More sympathetic critics find that the plays successfully embody
the author's intentions of dramatizing a synthesis of the two kinds of
motivation. Edward Murray, for instance, has made the same
observation as have Bentley and Mander, but in his view the difficulty of
branding Miller either a "social" or a "psychological" dramatist points to
a strength rather than to a flaw in his work: "At his best, Miller has
avoided the extremes of clinical psychiatric case studies on the one hand
and mere sociological reports on the other.... he has indicated ... how the
dramatist might maintain in delicate balance both personal and social
motivation."[5]

Miller himself has often spoken of modern drama in general and his own in particular in terms of a split between the private and the social. In the 1956 essay, "The Family in Modern Drama," he claims that the various forms of modern drama "express human relationships of a particular kind, each of them suited to express either a primarily familial relation at one extreme, or a primarily social relation at the other."[6] At times he has pointed to his own affinity with one or the other of these two extreme points of view on human relationships, as when he talks of the forties and fifties as "an era of gauze," for which he finds Tennessee Williams mainly responsible: "One of my own feet stands in this stream. It is a cruel, romantic neuroticism, a translation of current life into the war within the self. The personal has triumphed. All conflict tends to be transformed into sexual conflict."[7] More often, as in "The Shadow of the Gods," Miller has seen himself primarily in the social tradition of the Thirties. It is in this essay that Miller makes one of his most explicit statements on the need for a synthesis of the two approaches:

> Society is inside of man and man is inside society, and you cannot even create a truthfully drawn psychological entity on the stage until you understand his social relations and their power to make him what he is and to prevent him from being what he is not. The fish is in the water and the water is in the fish.[8]

Such synthesis, however, is fraught with problems which are closely connected with Miller's medium, the theater.

Indeed, for Miller synthesis has largely been a question of dramatic form, and the problem for the playwright has been to create a viable form that could bridge "the deep split between the private life of man and his social life." In addition to his frustration with audience responses and his desire to make himself more clearly understood, part of the momentum behind Miller's search for new and more satisfactory modes of expression after the realistic *All My Sons* has been the conviction that the realistic mode in drama was an expression of "the family relationship within the play" while "the social relationship within the play" evoked the "un-realistic modes."[9]

In retrospect Miller found that the theme of *All My Sons* (1947) "is the question of actions and consequences" (p. 20), and the play dramatizes this theme in the story of Joe Keller, for whom there was nothing bigger than the family, and his son Chris, for whom "one new thing was made" out of the destruction of the war: "A kind of—responsibility. Man for man" (p. 85). When Miller is slightly dissatisfied with his first successful play, it is because he believes that he had allowed the impact of what he calls one kind of "morality" to "obscure" the other kind "in which the play is primarily interested" (p. 18). These two kinds of "morality" are closely related to the two kinds of "motivation"—psychological and social—that John Mander and other critics have pointed to. The problem may be seen more clearly by observing that the play has two centers of interest. The one, in which Miller claims "the play is primarily interested," is intellectual, the other emotional. The former is mainly expressed through the play's dialogue, the latter is more deeply embedded in the action itself.

Joe Keller gradually emerges as a criminal. He has sold defective cylinder heads to the air force during the war and was thus directly responsible for the deaths of twenty-one pilots. The horror of this deed is further brought home to the audience by the discovery that Keller's elder son was a pilot lost in action. This is what we may call the emotional center of interest, and most of the plot is concerned with this past crime and its consequences for Keller and his family. But it is this emotional center that for Miller obscures the real meaning of the play.

Miller wanted his play to be about "unrelatedness":

> Joe Keller's trouble, in a word, is not that he cannot tell right from wrong but that his cast of mind cannot admit that he, personally, has any viable connection with his world, his universe, or his society.... In this sense Joe Keller is a threat to society and in this sense the play is a social play. Its "socialness" does not reside in its having dealt with the crime of selling defective materials to a nation at war—the same crime could easily be the basis of a thriller which would have no place in social dramaturgy. It is that the crime is seen as having roots in a certain relationship of the individual to society, and to a certain indoctrination he embodies, which, if dominant, can mean a jungle existence for all of us no matter how high our buildings soar.

(p. 19)

This, then, is the intellectual center of the play. Any good drama needs to engage the intellect as well as the emotions of its audience. Miller's problem is that these two spheres in *All My Sons* are not concentric. When a play has two centers of interest at odds with each other, the emotional one will often, as here, have a more immediate impact on the audience because it is more intimately related to the action of the play.[10] Invariably action takes precedence over the sophistication of dialogue or symbols.

Death of a Salesman (1949) may serve as further illustration of the point made about the two centers of interest in *All My Sons*. Bentley wrote that the key scene of the play could be the one in Howard Wagner's office or the one in the hotel room depending on whether the play was "political" or "sexual." There is no doubt, however, as to which scene has the greater impact in the theater. The hotel room scene is carefully prepared for. The constant references to stockings and the growing tension around the repeated queries about what had happened to Biff after he had gone to ask his father's advice in Boston are some of the factors that serve to high-light this scene. A more immediate impression is made on the audience by the mysterious laughter and the glimpse of a strange woman quite early in the first act. The point is, however, that it is primarily on the stage that this scene makes such an overwhelming impact that it tends to overshadow the other scenes that together make up the total image of Willy's plight. If the play is read, if one treats it as one would a novel, balance is restored and a good case may be made for a successful synthesis of "psychological" and "social" motivation as argued, for instance, by Edward Murray.[11]

Miller seems to have become increasingly aware of the difficulty of making a harmonious whole of his vehicle and his theme. His story would have sexual infidelity (consider for instance the prominence this factor must have in any brief retelling of the plot of *Death of a Salesman* or *The Crucible*) or another personal moral failure at its center, while the significance the story held for the author had to do with man's relationship to society, to the outside world. The one kind of "morality" continues to obscure the other. When starting out to write *A View from the Bridge* (1955), Miller had almost despaired of making himself understood in the theater: no "reviews, favorable or not," had mentioned what he had considered the main theme of *The Crucible* (1953). Since he, apparently, could not successfully merge his plots and his intended themes, he arrived at a scheme that on the face of it seems preposterous: he would "separate, openly and without concealment, the action of the next play, *A View from the Bridge*, from its generalized significance" (p. 47).

With such an attitude to the relationship between story and theme or "action" and "significance" there is little wonder that Miller was prone to writing plays where critics felt there was a conflict of themes. For while Miller's imagination generates plots along psychoanalytic lines, his intellect leans towards socio-economic explanations.

The story was, according to his own account, his starting point for *A View from the Bridge*:

> I had heard its story years before, quite as it appears in the play, and quite as complete.... It was written experimentally not only as a form, but as an exercise in interpretation. I found in myself a passionate detachment toward its story as one does toward a spectacle in which one is not engaged but which holds a fascination deriving from its monolithic perfection. If this had happened, and if I could not forget it after so many years, *there must be some meaning in it for me, and I could write what had happened, why it had happened, and to one side, as it were, express as much as I knew of my sense of its meaning for me. Yet I wished to leave the action intact so that the onlooker could seize the right to interpret it entirely for himself and to accept or reject my reading of its significance.*
>
> (pp. 47–48, my italics)

This decision, Miller explains, led to the creation of "the engaged narrator" (p. 47), the role played by Alfieri in *A View from the Bridge*.

The narrator is hardly an innovation in the history of dramatic literature, especially when seen in relation to the chorus in Greek drama. In our own time widely different playwrights like Thornton Wilder (*Our Town*) and Bertolt Brecht (*The Caucasian Chalk Circle*) have made successful use of the narrator. Such historical antecedents and the widespread use of narrators in modern drama should not be lost sight of when considering this aspect of Arthur Miller's plays. Miller's narrators, however, are closely connected with his reluctance to let his plays speak for themselves. They are born from his long and troubled struggle with dramatic form.

Arthur Miller had tried his hand at fiction as well as drama before he achieved success on Broadway with *All My Sons* in 1947. When he thought of his next play, his aim was to achieve "the density of the novel form in its interchange of viewpoints" (p. 30). Again and again he comments on *Death of a Salesman* in terms of a prose narrative, as when he contrasts its sense of time with that of *All My Sons*: "This time, if I could, I would have *told the whole story* and set forth all the characters in one unbroken speech or even one sentence or a single flash of light. As I look at the play now its form seems the form of a confession, for that is *how it is told* ..." (p. 24).[12] Although this may merely be a manner of speaking, as suggested by his own critique of the movie version where "drama becomes narrative" (p. 26), it does point to an attitude that in certain respects runs counter to drama: the story as something to be *told* as opposed to something to be *shown* or dramatised.

In fact, however, *Death of a Salesman* succeeds precisely because Willy's story is shown on the stage, not told. The possible uncertainty as to motivation does not detract from the intense and unified impact of the drama in the theater. The characters reveal themselves through action and dialogue supported by what Miller has called the play's "structural images" (p. 30). All the more striking then, the need Miller evidently felt to have the characters stand forth and give their various interpretations of Willy's life after the drama proper has closed with Willy's death. The chorus-like effect of the "Requiem" is obviously related to Miller's conscious effort to write a tragedy of "the common man," a drama which places man in his full social context, which in his essay "On Social Plays" is so clearly associated in Miller's mind with Greek drama. From another point of view the "Requiem" may also be seen as the embryo of the narrator figure who becomes so conspicuous in *A View from the Bridge* and *After the Fall*: after the play is over the characters stand forth and tell the audience what the play is about.

Miller's reluctance to let a play speak for itself became even more evident in his two attempts to add extra material to the original text of *The Crucible* after its first production in 1953. The first of these additions, a second scene in Act Two, helps to explain Abigail's behavior in Act Three, but, as Laurence Olivier told the playwright, it is not necessary.[13] Although Abigail's psychotic character is brought out entirely in action and dialogue, in an encounter with John Proctor on the eve of the trial, and there is no suggestion of extra-dramatic exposition, the added scene is nevertheless evidence of Miller's sense of not having succeeded in making himself understood in the original version of the play.

More striking is the evidence provided by the series of non-dramatic interpolated passages in the first act, where the playwright takes on the roles of historian, novelist and literary critic, often all at once, speaking himself *ex cathedra* rather than through his characters *ex scena*. There is an obvious difference in intent as well as effect in writing an introductory essay to one's play and writing a series of comments that are incorporated in the text itself. The material used need not be different. For example, some of the comments on Danforth in the "Introduction" to the *Collected Plays* are quite similar to those on Parris or Hale incorporated in the play. In the one instance, however, he is looking at his play from the outside, as one of its many critics, in the other he has added new material to the play and has thus changed the text.

In effect the play has a narrator, not realized as a character but present as a voice commenting on the characters and the action and making clear some of the moral implications for the reader/audience. The director of the 1958 Off Broadway revival of *The Crucible* drew the consequences of the revised text and introduced "a narrator, called The Reader, to set the scenes and give the historical background of the play."[14] Besides his function as one of the minor characters, this is what Alfieri does in *A View from the Bridge*. The introduction of a "narrator" element in *The Crucible* is closely related to Miller's attempts to have a separate voice present the author's view of the "generalized significance" of the "action" in the later play.

The interpolated expository passages of *The Crucible* serve two different purposes. Frequently the comments on a character merely repeat points made in that part of the drama which may be acted on the stage. Indeed, the opening words of the following paragraph on John Proctor are suggestive of the Victorian novelist guiding his readers through his story, making sure that no point, however obvious, may be missed:

> But as we shall see, the steady manner he displays does not spring from an untroubled soul. He is a sinner, a sinner not only against the moral fashion of the time, but against his own vision of decent conduct. These people had no ritual for the washing away of sins. It is another trait we inherited from

them, and it has helped to discipline us as well as to breed hypocrisy among us. Proctor, respected and even feared in Salem, has come to regard himself as a kind of fraud. But no hint of this has yet appeared on the surface, and as he enters from the crowded parlor below it is a man in his prime we see, with a quiet confidence and an unexpressed, hidden force. Mary Warren, his servant, can barely speak for embarrassment and fear.

(p. 239)

Proctor's sense of guilt is central to any understanding of him as a dramatic character, but certainly this is made sufficiently clear by, for instance, the several explicit remarks made by Elizabeth as well as by his behavior on the stage.

While such passages are further instances of Miller's apparent distrust of his medium as a means of communication, other passages speak of an impatience with the limitations of the dramatic form. Miller had researched this play thoroughly, and it is as if on second thought he has regretted that he had not been able to bring as much of his research and his historical insights into the play as he would have liked. But when he in the interpolated passages takes on the roles of historian and biographer he tends to confuse the sharp line that must be drawn between the characters in a play called *The Crucible* and a group of late seventeenth century individuals bearing the same names as these characters. Thus, in the first of the two paragraphs that serve to introduce Proctor as he enters on the stage, Miller tells us:

Proctor was a farmer in his middle thirties. He need not have been a partisan of any faction in the town, but there is evidence to suggest that he had a sharp and biting way with hypocrites. He was the kind of man—powerful of body, even-tempered, and not easily led—who cannot refuse support to partisans without drawing their deepest resentment. In Proctor's presence a fool felt his foolishness instantly—and a Proctor is always marked for calumny therefore.

(pp. 238–39)

The change in tense in the paragraph that follows (quoted above) suggests that Miller had a different Proctor in mind in each paragraph: the historical Proctor and the character in the play. This confusion runs through the various character sketches or brief essays on for instance Parris (pp. 225–29), Putnam (pp. 234–35) and Rebecca and Francis Nurse (pp. 242–43). It should further be noted that these interpolated expository passages are often concerned with motivation, and that both psychological, religious and socio-economic explanations of the trials are given. While the information is interesting in itself and throws light on the Salem trials, it cannot add to our understanding of the drama as acted on the stage. Whatever needs to be known about these characters and their motives by the audience must be expressed in action and dialogue. That is, if we do not accept the dichotomy of "action" and "significance," with the latter element presented by a representative of the author, a "Reader" or a narrator.

The assumption of such a dichotomy, according to Miller, lies at the heart of the structure of his next play, *A View from the Bridge*. Here, and in *A Memory of Two Mondays*, the one-act play originally presented on the same play bill, Miller thinks of himself as having followed "the impulse to present rather than to represent an interpretation of reality. Incident and character are set forth with the barest naïveté, and action is stopped abruptly while commentary takes its place" (p. 49). On the face of it, however, it is difficult to see why such commentary should be found necessary, unless the playwright had given up trying to make himself understood through "action" alone or, rather, to let his "action" carry the full weight of the "significance" he saw in it.

In his "Introduction" Miller claims at the outset that his "approach to playwriting and the drama itself is organic" (p. 3), and he insists that "the play must be dramatic rather than narrative in concept and execution" (p. 4). When towards the end of the "Introduction" he explains that "the organic impulse behind" his early plays was "split apart" in *A View from the Bridge*, it is as if he admits the failure of this approach. The organic structure of the early *All My Sons*, however, has already been questioned by Miller in his critique of its two centers of interest. As in this earlier play, the emotional center of *A View from the Bridge* is embedded in the action. But in the latter play Miller explains that he deliberately tried not to have the dialogue of the characters involved in the action carry any burden that goes beyond this action.

The aspect of the play that dialogue attempted to express in *All My Sons* is now delegated to the narrator. The more explicit splitting apart of "the organic impulse" has been observed in *Death of a Salesman* with its concluding "Requiem." Moreover, Miller has also been seen to depart from the second of his two basic principles of playwriting in introducing narrative and expository passages into *The Crucible*. With *A View from the Bridge* he wrote a play that approaches illustrated narrative.

Alfieri, the lawyer-narrator, opens the play by telling a little about himself and his neighborhood and suggesting some of the themes of the play to follow. When Eddie appears on the stage, the verbal tense Alfieri makes use of is striking in its implications: "This one's name *was* Eddie Carbone" (p. 379, my italics). Later in the play Alfieri consistently refers to Eddie in the past tense. The story is obviously Alfieri's story. What we see on the stage is Alfieri's memory of Eddie as he ponders on its significance: "This is the end of the story. Good night," he concludes the original one act version of the play.[15] The past tense is the mode of narrative; drama is enacted in the present.

The title *A Memory of Two Mondays* is in itself interesting in this connection as it suggests an implied narrator, someone whose memory is projected on the stage as is Alfieri's. This technique is developed to its furthest extreme in *After the Fall*, where "*the action takes place in the mind, thought, and memory of Quentin.*"[16] The play has become illustrated narrative, and is essentially a two act monologue which the narrator and main character Quentin, directs at the audience. Significantly, since the flow of narration is essential to the play and the many dramatizations of situations in the narrative are incidental, Quentin's audience is in Miller's stage directions defined as a "*Listener, who, if he could be seen, would be sitting just beyond the edge of the stage itself.*"[17]

The images presented on the stage are illustrations of Quentin's consciously controlled discourse or of the working of his sub-consciousness as he struggles for self-understanding and self-acceptance. In either case, the device of giving characters within "*the mind, thought, and memory of Quentin*" a semi-independent status on the stage and allowing them to speak for themselves, makes possible an objective view of the self-image projected by Quentin in his discourse. Essentially, however, Miller has placed a character on the stage and given him the opportunity of examining his life and motives and explaining himself to a Listener through a monologue that lasts the whole length of a two act play. From the point of view of genre the result is a cross between expressionist drama, stream of consciousness novel and dramatic monologue. The result, however, is good theater: it works on the stage. The critical attacks on *After the Fall* have mainly been concerned with Miller's subject matter and theme, not his experiment with dramatic form.

Rather than add a clarifying "Requiem," as he did with *Death of a Salesman*; rather than interpolate expository passages in the published play to make himself more readily understood, as he did in *The Crucible*; and rather than introduce a narrator, somewhat to the side of the central plot, who could explain the author's "reading of its significance," Miller in *After the Fall* made the narrator's attempt to arrive at the significance of his own life and explain himself directly to the audience the center of the play. Ironically, Miller may never have felt himself so misunderstood by audiences and critics alike as after the first production of *After the Fall* in 1964, the play that may be seen as the culmination of a series of efforts to develop a form that would allow him to present his intentions unmistakably and clearly to his public.

Some years earlier, in his "Introduction" to the *Collected Plays*, Miller had observed that "the intention behind a work of art and its effects upon the public are not always the same" (p. 8). His answers to the question of how to avoid this communication gap could not, finally, have struck him as successful in practice. In his next play, at least, *Incident at Vichy*, written immediately after the critical disaster of *After the Fall*, he returned to the form of the straightforward, realistic play. By concentrating on one of the two poorly integrated themes of *After the Fall*, that represented by the concentration camp tower, the later play, moreover, avoids the conflict between two different kinds of "morality" or "motivation" many critics have found in his plays up to and including *After the Fall*. *Incident at Vichy* may be too much the drama of ideas (and not very new or original ones at that) to be successful in the theater, and Von Berg's development may not be quite convincing on the stage; but at least there is no need for any "Requiem," explanatory footnotes or narrator to express the play's dominantly public theme.

Four years later Miller returned to the material of *All My Sons*, *Death of a Salesman* and *After the Fall* in another family drama, *The Price*. The play is also a return to the realistic style and retrospective technique of *All My Sons*. But of course Miller had traveled a long distance since 1947. There is a greater economy of characters and incidents, a more subtle and dramatically integrated use of symbols, no more need for manipulative, mechanistic devices like surprise arrivals or unsuspected letters. Two hours in an attic with old furniture and four people—and the experience in the theater is of something organic, something that comes alive and evolves before us on the stage. The playwright appears relaxed, confident that the "action" expresses its "generalized significance": the characters speak for themselves and the play speaks for Arthur Miller.[18]

The critics who found, I think rightly so, a confusion of private-psychological and public-political themes in Miller's plays were addressing themselves to the very Problem Miller has repeatedly pointed to as the central one for the dramatist in our day: how to create a form that can bridge "the deep split between the private life of man and his social life." Miller's belief, expressed in several essays in the mid-fifties, that it is the unrealistic modes of drama that are capable of expressing man's social relationships, as opposed to the realistic drama which is best suited to present the private life, is seen most clearly at work in *A View from the Bridge* from 1955. The "bridge," however, is rather crudely built: to the side of the realistic action stands the narrator, who in the first version of the play spoke in verse—poetry, according to Miller, being the style most closely related to public themes. In the light of such theories the author's misfired intentions with *After the Fall*, his most "unrealistic" play, may be more easily understood; and the irony of its reception as his most embarrassingly private play more readily appreciated. There is further irony in the successful synthesis of the public and the private spheres in *The Price*. For according to Miller's theory, the realism of this or any other play "could not, with ease and beauty, bridge the widening gap between the private life and the social life." But in his essay on "The Family in Modern Drama," Miller had also wondered: "Why does Realism always seem to be drawing us all back to its arms? We have not yet created in this country a succinct form to take its place."[19] This was written at a time when Miller was trying to break away from realism. This movement, however, had its temporary conclusion in *After the Fall*, the play that more than any other must have led Miller to despair of communicating his intentions to his audience.

The ironies of Arthur Miller's career as a dramatist were further compounded with the production of *The Creation of the World and Other Business* in 1973. In spite of the success, with audiences as well as with critics, of *The Price*, following the disastrous reception of his experiments in *After the Fall*, Miller seems unable to rest comfortably in the strong and protective arms of Realism. His latest play is his first attempt to express himself through comedy and pure fantasy, and in this his most radical departure from realism his earlier concern with the problems of integrating man's private and social life has given way to teleological speculation. Behind the fanciful cosmological draperies, however, one may discover the playwright's old story of the two sons and familial conflict. Indeed, the new play serves as a reminder that the Cain and Abel story is an archetypal pattern in *All My Sons, Death of a Salesman, After the Fall* and *The Price*.

In a different guise the old question of the two centers of interest is also raised by Miller's attempt at comedy. While God and Lucifer incessantly come together on the stage to discuss the Creator's design, Miller's alleged theme, the audience, who cannot but grow restless after two acts with God, his Angels and a boring couple named Adam and Eve, are finally given the two sons, the responsible and respected Cain and the irresponsible and loved Abel. The rather simplistic psychological presentation of the conflict between them is the kind of dramatic material Miller has successfully handled before, and both because it is welcome relief from the overall tediousness of the rest of the play and because it has dramatic potential, it will easily lay claim to the attention and the interest of the audience at the expense of the play's concern with the human dilemma. Miller's latest Broadway venture thus is not only thematically related to his first one but shows that the playwright has still not been able to solve the problem of dramatic form he then felt had served to obscure his main theme.

The story of Arthur Miller's struggle with dramatic form had its beginning in his realization of the two centers of interest in *All My Sons*. His subsequent theories of social drama and its relationship to the realistic and unrealistic modes of drama should be regarded primarily as rationalizations of his own attempts to express himself clearly, to bridge the gap not so much between the social and the private as between his conscious intentions and the audience and critical responses. This was fully demonstrated in his attempts deliberately to separate the action of a play from its significance. His distrust of the realistic drama as a usable medium was thus properly a distrust of the theater itself as a medium, as evidenced in his use of intermediary commentary and narrators and in his tendency towards illustrated narrative. Realism nevertheless has proved to have a strong hold on Miller, and it is the mode with which, the evidence of his plays suggests, he is most at home. *The Creation of the World and Other Business* marks a break with the tone and style of all his previous plays, but it is impossible at this point to guess whether it will turn out to be a new departure in his career or a dead end. Although Miller, like the devil in Ibsen's *Peer Gynt,* has not always been able to reckon with his audience, he has demonstrated that he has been extremely sensitive to their responses. He may therefore accept the common verdict of critics and audiences and return to the kind of work that has placed him in the front rank of contemporary dramatists.

NOTES

1. Quoted in Benjamin Nelson, *Arthur Miller: Portrait of a Playwright*, London, 1970, p. 320.

An early version of this essay was discussed in a seminar at the University of Bergen, Norway, and presented as a lecture at the Universities of Debrecen and Budapest, Hungary.

2. For instance: "in the writing of *Death of a Salesman* I tried, of course, to achieve a maximum power of effect. But when I saw the devastating force with which it struck its audiences, something within me was shocked and put off ... the emotionalism with which the play was received helped to generate an opposite impulse and an altered dramatic aim. This ultimately took shape in *The Crucible*...." "Introduction," *Collected Plays*, New York, 1957, p. 38. Page references in parentheses are to this edition.

3. *What is Theatre? Incorporating the Dramatic Event and Other Reviews 1944–1967*, New York, 1968, p. 261.

4. London, 1961, p. 151.

5. *Arthur Miller: Dramatist*, New York, 1967, p. 180. Compare Sheila Huftel, *Arthur Miller: The Burning Glass*, New York, 1965, p. 60: "the synthesis of social and psychological in *After the Fall* has always been with him, the cornerstone on which his plays are built."

6. *The Atlantic Monthly* 197, April 1956, p. 35.

7. Henry Brandon, "Sex, Theater, and the Intellectual: A Conversation with Marilyn Monroe and Arthur Miller," *As We Are*, New York, 1961, p. 125.

8. "The Shadow of the Gods: a Critical View of the American Theatre," *Harper's Magazine* 217, August 1958, p. 39. A similar statement is made in the "Introduction" to the *Complete Plays*, p. 30.

9. "The Family in Modern Drama," pp. 40, 36. Miller often returns to this point, for instance in the essay "On Social Plays," published as an introduction to *A View from the Bridge*, London, 1957, where he refers to "prose realism" as "the one form that was made to express the private life," and writes of the "struggle taking place in the drama today—a struggle at one and the same time to write of private persons privately and yet lift up their means of expression to a poetic— that is, a social—level." (pp. 7–8)

10. Raymond Williams has made a similar point in his *Drama from Ibsen to Brecht*, London, 1968, p. 270: "The words ... expressing Keller's realization of a different kind of consciousness, have to stand on their own, because unlike the demonstration of ordinary social responsibility they have no action to support them, and moreover as words they are limited to the conversational resources so adequate elsewhere in the play, but wholly inadequate here to express so deep and substantial a personal discovery (and if it is not this it is little more than a maxim, a 'sentiment')."

11. This is in fact the way in which Murray arrives at his evaluation. Discussing *The Crucible* he writes, "The crucial question, however, is: Does Miller succeed in fusing the 'personal' and the 'social'? A close reading of the play would suggest that he does." (p. 73)

12. My italics. Compare phrases like "The way of telling the tale ..." (p. 26) and "the form the story would take." (p. 31)

13. See Arthur Miller, *The Crucible*, ed. by Gerald Weales, New York, 1971. Olivier's remark is quoted in "A Note on the Text," pp. 153–54. The extra scene is printed in an appendix. It was first published in the edition of the play that appeared in *Theatre Arts* 37, October 1953.

14. *Ibid.*, p. 169n.

15. Quoted from the periodical version, *Theatre Arts* 40, September 1956.

16. New York, 1964, p. 1.

17. *Ibid.*, p. 2.

18. The "Author's Production Note" to *The Price* may suggest, however, that Miller still was not entirely confident that he had succeeded in making himself understood. He takes care to explain that

"A fine balance of sympathy should be maintained in the playing of the roles of Victor and Walter," as if the text itself does not make clear that "both men" are presented "in all their humanity and from their own viewpoints." He even finds it necessary to give his view of the theme of the play: "As the world now operates, the qualities of both brothers are necessary to it; surely their respective psychologies and moral values conflict at the heart of the social dilemma." (London, 1968, p. [117])

19. "The Family in Modern Drama," pp. 40, 36.

MARIANNE BORUCH

Miller and Things

We are faced with a crowd of things: a cracked cylinder head from an old P-40, a copper pot, silk stockings pressed and gleaming in their cardboard box. We spot a harp, its baseboard somewhat warped yet still quite impressive, golden against a monsterous bureau, or over there, a pile of auto parts: crankshafts, engine pins, grimy axles. Perhaps in the distant left, that's a real tower, dark and frightening, the barbed wire fringe from a past—or future—time. An old radio sits in the dust, and near it, a newspaper curled tightly and torn—in anger?—then dropped. Here's a simple chair, there, a fencer's foil and mask, a football, a fountain pen. We walk around these things, among them; they make an American ruin, a junkyard of moments and desires, fascinating in themselves, but absurd. How does one pull these things into a human focus? The job seems enormous, impossible.

Yet think of the wheelwright, the shipwright. The playwright, is he really any different? Does not this joiner take human and inanimate substance and "work" them together toward some larger end? It was Willy Loman who stated with sudden coherence that, "if a man can't handle tools he's not a man."[1] In speaking of drama, one could widen the remark and venture that a playwright is not a good playwright unless he can take the hard, physical extension of our ideas—things, objects—and use them dramatically, as pivots of human action and revelation. But

From *The Literary Review*, vol. 24, no. 4. ©1981 by Fairleigh Dickinson University. Reprinted by permission.

more than that, one could say a playwright is not a great playwright unless he can use things—in themselves—thematically, not simply as properties to be touched then discarded on the way to discovery, but somehow as the discovery itself. At this point, drama extends itself into poetry, and metaphor swells with movement to a broader, historical reality. Arthur Miller operates in this vision with reserve and intelligence and surprise.

He operates such power initially. The touch of any world begins, of course, with what we first see; and in Miller's opening stage demands, we not only find the physical setting depicting time and place, we often are presented with objects that instruct us intuitively through their metaphoric quality. In *All My Sons*, for instance, Miller stages the house and backyard to a kind of Norman Rockwellian perfection, yet the vital element in the setting is the yard's single apple tree, left broken and lifeless by the savage force of the previous night's storm. All opening conversation moves in one way or another around this freak event, and we learn quickly that the tree is more than just a tree. It represents— quite consciously to the characters—the life of the young man, Larry, reported to be missing-in-action, whom some mourn and whom others hope still lives. We realize the intensity of the latter belief because a tree is a hopeful memorial, alive and fruitful; and that a mother should run out into the dark, wet middle of the night to stand in a mute despair at its destruction—as she is reported to have done—immediately presses into icon a rich tension of feeling which is almost effortlessly dramatic. It might be a weak, frivolous idea to structure all action around a missing character, but Miller has solved any possible problem by offering a hard symbolic replacement, thus making such absence seem in fact more powerful than the living presence could probably be. But the tree reveals more. Somewhere in our image-recording subconscious an important seed has been planted. Amid the house and yard and the successful, happy Kellers, seemingly launched full sail into the American dream, something is wrenched and terribly wrong. The only living thing on the place has been broken, suddenly and in darkness split by a broad and violent fact. And we grasp in some strange, inarticulate way that the action will move mysteriously toward revelation of this buried vitality.

Sometimes there is little such mystery about Miller's opening images. As we enter *Death of a Salesman*, witnessing the pressure of those "towering angular shapes" of apartments upon Willy's "fragile-seeming house," the situation seems clear. Hope is losing, and all of the battle will be a sad, desperate business. The apartments appear cool and rational—"a solid vault"—with the self-possession and heartless intention of human manipulators. Through his deliberate staging, drawing the outside world cold and cruel against the inside home "with an air of a dream," Miller has set Willy's point of view indelibly on the reality we are entering. Things brood here, and they break, yet there is possible goodness in that house. As the light takes over the stage, the apartment sky glows its "angry orange" while the Loman house and the forestage are bathed in the frank, simple "blue light of the sky" (D. 11). The two realities exist so far from each other, they have assumed different weather. In this contrast, we instantly feel the weight on Willy's life and realizations; and by the power of the stage images, his helpless exhaustion that opens the play strikes us as more than believable; it seems inevitable.

A similar view operates in the short play *A Memory of Two Mondays*, as Miller works toward an atmosphere partly physically real, partly felt. Yet here the division becomes harder to express imagistically because things move within the location completely; no large, clear comparisons like "outside" and "inside" can be ascertained. Yet the warehouse loft is "surrounded"[2] on all sides by enormous floor-to-ceiling windows, windows ordinarily for light and real world air and color. But these are shut and so encrusted with years of dust that they allow nothing to enter or escape. Everything endures in a strange mix of possibility and oppressive fact. If Miller, in *Death of a Salesman*, had originally wanted the set to be built, literally, in the shape of a skull, the shape of Willy thinking and dreaming back, we have in this set a semi-realization of that wish, a skull-like enclosure, sealed, and thus free-floating in time—indeed, like memory itself.

Personal history is often thus sealed, the chaos of people and things flattened in an inescapable airless room in the back of thought. Nowhere is this idea made so immediately concrete as in the opening vision of *The Price*. For a long, lean minute, the room itself is the dramatic event—people are elsewhere; and Miller instructs that the place be "progressively seen."[3] One imagines the growing attention of the audience as the beam slowly moves off the cozy, almost natural situation of center stage with its flowered armchair and end table and old twenties radio, moving now in a larger and larger circle of light to include the monstrous bulk of stuff—furniture, clothing, keepsakes—everything hoarded over a lifetime. In a minute, Victor Franz will arrive to deal with the evaluation of these objects, and his life, but it seems a masterful stroke to leave us in the problem first-hand, and by that experience we come to the action aware and ready and perhaps, sympathetic.

Just as Miller manipulates objects with the hope of bringing us logically and intuitively into the beginning dramatic action, so he takes care to sustain our interest by discreet use of his powerful techniques throughout the body of the play. In all his work, action rises and falls, sometimes slowly, sometimes abruptly, and often he calls our attention to a special moment by the emphatic use of an ordinary object. Perhaps the finest example of such procedure comes before and after the famous boxing "lesson" in *A View from the Bridge*. Working himself up to fight, Eddie underpins his offensive ramble concerning Rodolpho's inability on the waterfront with the unconscious violent twisting of a rolled newspaper which suddenly tears in two; and Miller stage whispers, "they are all regarding him now."[4] With them, we begin to see the new Eddie as a kind of monster. Under this light, the scene plays with an inarticulate tension pulsing just below the surface, building upward to the act's final stunning gesture of power and warning and—not surprisingly—prophecy. Seemingly a game of strength, Marco's game turns, and Eddie finds himself stuck helpless, a large chair poised menacingly over his head. Act one ends with a terrifying silence as they absorb each other's look under the dark shadow of the extraordinary weapon.

Miller has a fondness for such ritualistic gestures, especially to close out important action. In *All My Sons*, act one ends with a charged conversation between Joe and his wife, who questions George's motivation in coming for a visit. "Be Smart," Kate repeats in a fearful litany as Joe moves about the stage, angry, frightened and then truly desperate. "Be smart," she says, her final warning and plea, and as if in response, Keller "in hopeless fury, looks at her, turns around ... slamming the screen door violently behind him."[5] One imagines the sound of that door haunting the entire intermission. Unlike Marco's chair-raising which ends act one in *A View from the Bridge* and seems delivered "in-character," a non-verbal expression of power and dignity, Keller's violence here creates a startling discovery. A man normally talkative, good-natured and friendly has clearly been forced back abruptly, into a dark, confused corner of himself. The slamming of the door not only ends the act; it ends the old Keller we saw moving in act one. Suddenly, we perceive something new, a deeper tension in the play, as Keller, too, discovers something, a darker creature stirring within.

There are softer ways to eclipse great movement in Miller's world. In *Death of a Salesman*, act one ends in a kind of double exposure as Miller stages two scenes quietly in tandem. A conversation occurs between Willy and Linda upstairs while Biff wanders around in the nighttime kitchen. A rather stunning visual effect takes place, with Miller playing the verbal against its opposite. The pensive Biff comes downstage, the glow of his smoking cigarette circling him in the darkness as Willy softly reminisces about the Ebbets field game. "[Biff was] like a young god. Hercules—something like that. And the sun, the sun all around him ..." (D. 68). Miller often uses the slow, smoking cigarette to express a kind of thoughtfulness and solitary feeling in his characters. At the outset of act two, in *After the Fall*, Quentin also is moving in darkness and "a spark is seen, a flame fires up ... he is discovered lighting his cigarette."[6]

Things do not simply end and begin when the playwright sections off movement into acts and scenes. Often there are shifts of power between characters, realizations of broader, more frightening factors underpinning gesture and remark, confrontations which in one way or another turn dramatic event but do not lie easily discernible in the minute or two before intermission. Although coming near the end of the play, Ann's letter from Larry in *All My Sons* illustrates the gigantic effect of a single object on the meaning of anything previously enacted. The scene is powered like a nightmare game of "telephone." Each character, as he or she absorbs the message, is savagely torn out of innocence, real or imagined, and launched into a sadder, more complex but philosophically larger world.

Less the total cause of realization and more the supporting evidence in the difficult journey toward it, a rubber hose in *Death of a Salesman* becomes both a symbol of Willy's profound wish for release and, in Biff's hands, a potent psychological weapon. When he finally finds his truth and begins its painful articulation near the play's end, Biff flings down the hose to force Willy's deepest attention, shouting, "all right, phoney! Then let's lay it on the line" (D. 130). By mixing gesture, object and language, Miller signals us on a rational and on an instinctual level into an interaction not previously attempted in the play.

Meanwhile, buried in the structure of the first act of *The Price*, a quieter kind of shift is taking place. The object here is an old tubey radio, one loaded with personal meaning for Victor, who assembled it as a boy. He and Esther have been sparring, and Victor, withdrawing, hurt, notices the radio under other furniture. For Miller, such action is never arbitrary. At a particular moment of marital un-bliss, Victor's discovery—a machine whose only purpose is to receive or transmit bits of human affairs—points us to another matter. Victor has gotten "the message," he says. "Like what?" Esther fearfully asks. "What other message is there?" he answers (P. 362), pulling out the radio with sudden absorption. And Esther, wanting desperately to make the "contact" Miller encourages in the stage notes, begins her polite questions concerning the radio itself. When dealing with characters as shy and gentle as Miller clearly perceives Esther and Victor to be, the playwright often focuses on a cover interest while actually involved with a far deeper probe. Because of the radio, he is able to operate discreetly, on almost a totally symbolic level, which permits us to see both the evasion and understanding active in the relationship of the characters we are viewing.

Miller's imagination holds other, more obvious tricks. Both the repetition of the flute music and the reappearing angular presence of the apartments give notice throughout *Death of a Salesman* of serious intensity at work. The former device enters at moments when Willy feels especially drawn to a vision of past hopes and we sense freedom in his dream, a frontier rich-quick grace we can imagine in the music itself. The latter lights up menacingly when Willy feels haunted, overburdened, hopeless. "They boxed us in here. Bricks and windows, bricks and windows ..." (D. 17). A similar thing, of course, happens in *After the Fall*, the horrible tower looming its guilty, historical weight above Quentin's head throughout the play. Willy Loman, too, is caught in his own inescapable cycle of guilt. But predictably, his is little, personal. He can't get rid of the ghost of silk stockings, symbol of his infidelity, and thus, cause of Biff's distrust. It is simply amazing to me that whole years of experience and emotion can be caught in a single object and flung into the text so potently. It strikes me as powerful partly because it is the way memory works. Such gestures give a psychological clarity and texture to motivation that we recognize instantly. It is almost as if Miller has told us a story so well, he needs only to mention one aspect of its delivery for us to gather its full force again, and be moved.

But he knows greater symbolic tricks. With well-chosen objects Miller tips us off to the inner substance of his characters, or at least what they appear to be to the main figures whose viewpoints often shadow the plays. Holga, for instance, in *After the Fall*, is continually directed to hold flowers, at one point wanting to fill the whole car with them and, one foresees, Quentin's questioning, colorless life. During Willy Loman's hopeful moments in *Death of a Salesman*, Linda is cheerful and young, forever entering and exiting with ribbons in her hair, perpetually the "good sport" smiling over the laundry. People should, perhaps, be judged by their highest thoughts, their kindest behavior, but in Miller's world, and ours, they *are* what they hold, or wear, or buy or want. In *A View from the Bridge*, Eddie at first allegedly objects only to Rodolpho's fondness for what he considers transient and flashy items—motorcycles, records, the bright glitter of Broadway. Of course, he has deeper motives for his distaste, but Eddie feels comfortable listing his reasons in concrete, seemingly rational terms, just as we feel comfortable and omniscient seeing through them. Objects, in Miller's hands, are often a lens into the rather murky business of making characters rounder and fuller and finally, living. We get to the point quickly that way; relation is set up and we can get on with the changes that larger drama promises.

But what is that larger promise? Here, probably, is the basic question one circles endlessly when discussing the impressive bundle of work some playwrights have produced. Miller undoubtedly handles his objects with discrimination and power on a theatrical level—how scenes themselves "play," when and how characters find and test their options in the social muddle of duty and affection—all these patterns wind themselves up and down around the natural orientation of things. Bits of the real world we find so convincing on the stage seem to be "real toads in imaginary gardens." Or just real pegs to hang a coat on. One can say Miller is a "great" playwright because when using these tools or toads or pegs, he takes them beyond mere mechanics into thematic richness. His only problem might be that he started too large.

Chris, for instance, seems enormous. The moral bullet, the boy who loves his father, the man who "makes people want to be better" (S. 395), this is the Chris who opens act two of *All My Sons*. We find him stripped to the waist, a young, hard-working god-man sawing the splintered apple tree into firewood oblivion. Although this is reasonable enough—after all, who wouldn't get rid of the glaring memorial to the brother whose girlfriend one wants to marry?—the scene strikes a bit false. Something is wrong—the mythic touch of apple, the innocent young man trying to remove the violent matter in the twilight following the storm; something feels bigger than life here, but its power is confused and derivative. By this gesture, of course, Chris takes control of what happens ever after, but the amplification loses him his human edge. He becomes symbol, or "the statue" a neighbor—Sue—insists he dangerously is. In short, we are looking at a thing: a static predictable creation to whom people react in predictable ways.

Yet Chris's reification can be defended as a crucial part of the thematic structure of *All My Sons*. Some people are things, Miller seems to suggest, but finally realizing the cruel complexity of the world, as Chris does by the play's end, they become somehow human again, and by the transformation, are able to see others as equally failed, thus rounded, humans. After his fall from innocence, Chris does indeed claim to understand his father not as a father, but as a man.

Other people in Miller's world never evolve out of their "thingdom": a few of the women, for instance. In *All My Sons*, Ann walks into the Kellers' and is seen as a bubble, a threat or a promise. She is quickly maneuvered by everyone into the hair-thin position between realities past and future, becoming as the action progresses the unsettling agent of reexamination and change. But Ann herself never changes. George enters to name her with accuracy. "She's one item you're not going to have" (S. 407). In the static center of the play's painful bargain for truth, she waits to be developed.

Often Miller uses his "thing characters" temporarily, for small effect in characterizing more important figures, much as a painter adds a side blur of color to create a setting for what he really sees. Happy, the cavalier Loman in *Death of a Salesman*, speaks of ladies as if their pursuit were a game, like bowling. "I just keep knocking them down ..." (D. 25). Quentin, in *After the Fall*, might agree. "Why do I keep sniffing the past?" he asks. "Except—there did seem some duty in the sky. I had a dinner table and a wife—a child ..." (F. 17). That particular wife, Louise, claims what he wanted was a comforter, a worshipper. "I'm not a praise machine" (F. 44), she objects. Yet there is little in the text itself to make her develop beyond the one-layered grouch she appears to be in

Quentin's presence. She remains, for us, a thing, a machine—perhaps not a praise machine, as she says, but a flat figure who exists only to show us another avenue into Quentin. The thematic point in using such shorthand for Louise and others is that through that sketching, the main characters are developed into the kinds of figures who actually see people in terms of their usefulness in a specific world. Happy and Quentin make their egocentricities more and more apparent as one "thing" leads to another. In Happy's case, it is a natural leap from a man who treats women as nighttime toys to the man who could walk out on his hysterical father in a public place, claiming it's not his father at all, but just "a guy" (D. 115).

The situation of Catherine in *A View from the Bridge* illustrates an odd plotting idea in the wider, thematic use of things. To ruin Rodolpho in her eyes, Eddie insists she is simply a passport ticket for him, American bait, just a useful item to be discarded as soon as citizenship opens. It seems an effective argument at first because Rodolpho is presented as an enthusiastic collector of glamorous objects carrying little value beyond the moment they fill. It becomes clear, however, that Eddie's understanding is a bit reversed. It is he who views Catherine possessively, as a thing to be, at least psychologically, had and controlled. It is Eddie who becomes the angry god watching his handiwork drop down the drain. He tells Alfieri, "I worked like a dog twenty years so a punk could have her?" (B. 60)

Miller handles a similar idea in his later play, *The Creation of the World*. But here, the angry god is a real god and the handiwork kicked downstairs to the waiting Satan is man—in toto—mankind. Perhaps this is the largest working of things thematically: people are not only manipulated by forces grander, more knowing than themselves, they are invented by them. This seems just more obvious and not too far from, say, a Willy Loman who invents a specific Ben in his imagination so he will have a hiding place when hope dies in the real, outer world. But in *Creation*, people have refused to act like things, or at least they have refused god's peculiar version of how human things should behave. For this, they are condemned out of perfection, out of Paradise and thrust into a difficult, weary life.

The life of a Willy Loman? Paradise evaporates and is that what awaits us on the barren plain? In its eerie and powerful movement, perhaps *Death of a Salesman* makes Miller's most ambitious attempt at defining twentieth-century man caught in western, industrial confusion. As we are guided through Willy's splintering reality, we catch sight of the vast, oppressive clutter which weighs so heavily on his world, reducing it—at least in Miller's eyes—to meaninglessness.

Item one: everything is breaking down. If it's not the refrigerator, it's the car or the washing machine or the vacuum cleaner. "I'm always in a race with the junkyard" (D. 73), Willy complains. But more than just objects seem to be flying apart. The salesman's dream of a world where experienced old men keep their power, sitting in robe and velvet slippers in hotel suites, dialing in thousands of sales in a single morning, is a fantasy that comes crashing around Willy almost audibly as he quarrels with Howard for a less exhausting job. It is a highly symbolic scene, almost unbearable to read or watch because Howard, faced with his human machine and his inhuman one, clearly prefers the latter. Before the suffering Willy, he is oblivious, cheerfully possessed with his new toy, the tape recorder clicking on and off, bringing the voices of his family grotesquely into the room.

Such monstrous thoughtlessness turns people into even less than things. Willy argues against the assumption, pointing to years of hard work, and loyalty and fatherly affection as evidence of his personal worth. "A man is not a piece of fruit," he exclaims. "You can't eat the orange and throw the peel away" (D. 82). But Howard is unconcerned with his appetite or his manners, as are, by implication, the millions like him in positions of power in industrial America. To such intelligence, people are, first to last, tools, useful toward production, toward profit. Beyond that, they are not even pathetic, they are invisible.

The scene in the office ends with a terrible meaning. Howard leaves the room, and Willy slips into a fantasy plea to Howard's dead father, who once owned the firm. As he leans over the desk, arms imploring, he accidentally clicks on the tape recorder and jumps back, terrified of its life: the ridiculous rendition of states and their capitals in a child's nasal voice. "Howard!" Willy screams in near breakdown, "Howard!" as if left alone and helpless in the room with a killer.

Such a killer mysteriously haunts the sealed-windowed set of *A Memory of Two Mondays* as well. We hear of a dark, dense area above the warehouse room, full of bins, the bins stuffed with used auto parts: mufflers and Marmon valves, ignitions, differentials, Locomobile headnuts. We can imagine blackened treasures no one remembers or cares to remember, parts of a whole almost impossible to understand. The weight of this room presses on the action, the physical presence of industrial complexity multiplied to madness. Under it, Gus's desperate litany of his long years with the place seems especially poignant. Who will remember him? Times themselves are no longer known because of their people, but because of the machines those people produce. Gus's realization forces him back to a final dream: to die flashy and well.

That final dream remains crucial to Miller and the visual, concrete form it takes in his hands makes, especially in *Death of a Salesman*, for stunning and memorable theater. After rejection by both Howard and his son, Willy purchases seeds—carrots, peas, beets, lettuce—and proceeds by flashlight in the middle of the night to plant them. "Nothing's planted. I don't have a thing in the ground" (D. 122), he worries, buying them, the remark multiplying to reflect upon his whole life of work and love. But as he gets happily to the job, he begins his mad discourse with the make-believe Ben, planning for a logical, lucrative suicide. It seems fitting that such painful thinking should take place in the garden: real earth, solid earth inviting essential meditation as the human world sags apart. We feel instinctively that Miller's choice of the whole business—the seeds, the hoe, even the darkness—is terrifyingly correct and implies a despair no longer even social, but now, desperately solitary. It represents Willy's and perhaps our own deepest wish back to the simplicity and the cyclical wholeness gardens symbolize, and the move comes with great power now in sudden contrast to the abstract complexities and cruelties of urban spirit. In this dense inner world, Willy yearns to grasp the real, the concrete and, through that, the release as Ben more and more lures him with diamonds, diamonds. "I can see it," Willy says, "shining in the dark, hard and rough, that I can pick up and touch with my hand. Not like—like an appointment!" (D. 126)

Yet, in Miller's world, even dreams become absurd, their baggage at last, heavy and silly and seemingly impossible to get rid of. Willy's dream land of big games and diamond mines and assistant buyer positions might be more beautiful than his actual everyday life, but as Biff slowly realizes, its self-inflation is eventually fatal. Such a revelation holds us abruptly in *The Price* as the playwright forces us face to face with the accumulation of the past, both of its dream and reality life. How overwhelming it seems! How monstrous. Here the bulk of furniture and keepsakes functions as an enormous lens through which Victor and Walter see and awkwardly refocus their lives, each examining the other's assumptions the way Solomon goes about evasively, stubbornly sizing up the unwanted pieces.

Yet the evaluation can't be final; it is already a draw, a stalemate. Who can be right anymore, Miller seems to ask. Furniture once chosen with care and pride now strikes the world as more than ridiculous— useless—not even the proper size to slip through the doorways of current apartments. Solomon informs us that it is all a matter of viewpoint, that this is a disposable world of shortsightedness and second chances. Victor himself tells us "it's impossible to know what's important. You shovel the crap out the window, it comes back under the door" (P. 384). In such a world, how are we to judge anything, any person, any self?

Perhaps the best we can hope for is perspective, a touch of Solomon's humor to soften the edge of things real, or imagined. As the appraiser stalks through the set, he seems new, coming not to a flattened despair, but to life in the American ruin of complexity and greed. He sees philosophically, with an historical rush of intention and acceptance. Such a freedom frees us, and in Solomon's simple, saving moments it is Miller flashing his genius from the dark gloom of the clutter.

NOTES

1. Arthur Miller, *Death of a Salesman* (New York: Penguin Books, 1976), p. 44. All citations from Miller's plays after the initial identifying footnote will follow the cited passage in parentheses and preceded by an identifying initial: D, *Death of a Salesman*; M, *A Memory of Two Mondays*; P, *The Price*; B, *A View from the Bridge*; S, *All My Sons*; F, *After the Fall*.

2. Arthur Miller, *A Memory of Two Mondays*, The Viking Press (1955), rpt. in *One Act*, ed. Samuel Moon (New York: Grove Press, 1961), p. 253.

3. Arthur Miller, *The Price*, in *The Portable Arthur Miller* (New York: Penguin Books, 1977), p. 345.

4. Arthur Miller, *A View from the Bridge* (New York: Bantam Books, 1961), p. 70.

5. Arthur Miller, *All My Sons*, in *Six Great Modern Plays* (New York: Dell Books, 1956), p. 391.

6. Arthur Miller, *After the Fall* (New York: Bantam Books, 1965), p. 83.

HELGE NORMANN NILSEN

From Honors at Dawn *to* Death of a Salesman: Marxism and the Early Plays of Arthur Miller

During the period from the nineteen-thirties through the forties
Marxism exercised a controlling influence on Arthur Miller's work. This
is evident in several of his earliest, unpublished plays, propaganda pieces
advocating the overthrow of capitalism and the establishment of a
socialist system.[1] The political tendency of these plays is too obvious to
be ignored, but it has escaped the attention of most readers that the same
message is embodied in the first three plays that Miller published. These
are *The Man Who Had All the Luck* (1944), *All My Sons* (1947) and *Death
of a Salesman* (1949), his most famous work.

   If one compares the unpublished plays with the published ones, the
common features emerge. American capitalism is criticized and rejected,
and an alternative, socialist community and system of values are pointed
to. The message is implicit rather than explicit in the printed works, but
the political agenda remains the same. The most important reason
behind Miller's commitment to radicalism is that the Great Depression
created in him a lasting and traumatic impression of the devastating
power of economic forces in the shaping of people's lives. This also
meant that, in the early plays, he portrayed and analyzed his major
characters as products of the American capitalist society and its
influence.[2] At the same time he managed to give them individuality and
persuasiveness as characters.

From *English Studies: A Journal of English Language and Literature*, vol. 75, no. 2. ©1994 by
Swets & Zeitlinger. Reprinted by permission.

Miller's political attitudes at the time emerge mainly in the plays in question, but are also described in his autobiography. They fall within the tradition of analysis and criticism of capitalism established by Marx and the movements building on his theories. Miller's critique can be summed up as follows: capitalism is inhuman in its glorification of private property and its exclusive orientation toward profitmaking. Human beings are sacrificed to economic interests in ways that are not only immoral, but even criminal in nature. In business, ruthless competition is the norm. People's moral character is threatened. They may become scoundrels, or rendered insane and suicidal. Egocentric individualism reigns supreme, and society fosters no sense of responsibility to anyone beyond self and family. There is an unjust concentration of financial power into a few hands, making all others powerless and bereft of economic security. The capitalists also control most of the cultural life of society and the media, spreading their conservative political views. No institution or aspect of society can escape this influence. The false values of materialism and the cult of success threaten to extinguish human love and caring. Conformism rules, turning people into mere cogs in the machine of production, and genuine individualism and even enjoyment of life become hard to obtain. The coming socialist society, on the other hand, will be built on solidarity, human brotherhood and the ownership of the workers and citizens of the means of production.[3]

In *Honors at Dawn*, dated 1937, the twenty-two-year old Miller launches one of his first attacks on capitalism. The setting, appropriately enough, is a factory where the workers have gone on strike to get a pay rise as well as recognition of their trade union. A typical class struggle follows in which the capitalists refuse to yield any ground to those who have to sell their labor to them. The main characters are two brothers, Max and Harry Zibriski, and the latter plans to become an engineer, believing that the key to success and security is education. But he is disabused of this notion by Smygli, a worker who articulates Miller's view of capitalism as an inherently unstable system: 'You think because you carry a T square and a slide rule the world will let you in peace? Forget it.'[4] In this system, no one is safe. Everyone is subject to the capricious rule of the laws of capitalism, and the workers are alienated, in the Marxist sense. They have been deprived of any genuine, personal relation to the production process.

Honors at Dawn also illustrates how the owners of capital extend their influence beyond the factory door. Max and Harry eventually attend the university, but there they realize that Mr. Castle, the plant owner, is in a position to bend the university administration to his will because he donates money to the institution. He tells its president that radical teachers must be fired so that students are not exposed to their influence. In the Marxist terms which Miller surely knew, the ruling ideas are the ideas of the ruling class. They constitute the false consciousness that only the politically aware can see through. Max is one of these, and disgusted by what he has experienced, he goes back to the plant, determined to do his part in the class struggle.[5]

In *The Great Disobedience*, another manuscript play, the subject is the conditions and functions of prisons under capitalism. A prison psychiatrist, Dr. Mannheim, is not allowed to make decisions concerning the treatment of the prisoners. They are regarded as expendable items whose rehabilitation is not cost-effective. The institution is itself corrupt, the guards selling narcotics to the inmates. The influence of the capitalists extends not only into the university, but into the prison as well. Mr. Riker, a wealthy manufacturer, persecutes a prisoner and sees to it that he is put into a maximum security cell. The man had worked for Riker and had threatened to expose his mistreatment of his employees.

Mannheim at first refuses to realize that people outside of the prison system can control it. He has not yet learnt the basic tenet of Marxism, that all power is ultimately economic. He believes that the institutions of society are divided into separate compartments, as it were: prisons here, factories there, and so on. To the Marxist, however, it is evident that all the institutions, or parts, of capitalist society are organized in such a way that they serve the interests of the ruling class.

But Mannheim gradually realizes what is going on and succeeds in putting McLean, a deputy warden, behind bars for running a drug racket in the prison. He resolves to improve the conditions and make the jail more like a hospital, with rehabilitation as its goal. Then it will become a model institution: 'The world is going to America for the best system ... We'll make the Russians look like amateurs.'[6] At this early stage, the Soviet Union could still function as an ideal society for Miller and other American radicals. In contrast, America is a place where 'one man is owned by another like a beast is owned.'[7] The root cause of this social evil is private ownership, which makes it possible for one man to be another's employer. Mannheim finally decides to continue the fight against capitalism, having understood the workings of the system.

Miller's unpublished works also include several versions of one and the same play, called variously *No Villain*, *The Grass Still Grows* or *They Too Arise*. The first manuscript dates from 1935 and is called both *The Grass Still Grows* and *They Too Arise*. It can be regarded as the origin of both *All My Sons* and *Death of a Salesman*, and it presents the typical Miller family for the first time, mother, father, two sons and a daughter. In later versions the daughter was dropped. The text, which is quite short and rudimentary, shows monopoly capitalism at work. The small businessmen, like Abe Simon, the main character, are being squeezed out by the bigger ones, who can offer lower prices. Then they take over the market. They are also ready to use violence against striking workers. Abe and his sons, Ben and Arnold, take a final stand against this system and its methods, Abe declaring that his offspring 'ain't gonna get rich by killing.'[8]

The succeeding versions of this play were considerably expanded. In one of them, also called *The Grass Still Grows*, the harshness of the conditions of the workers in the New York garment industry is exposed. As for Abe Simon, he now tries to solve his economic problems by getting Ben to marry a rich girl, who in later versions appears as Helen Roth. However, Abe is beginning to understand that it is morally wrong for a person to marry for money.

This play ends happily, with both sons married to women they love. As Abe says: 'They got the main thing,' meaning love.[9] Instead of struggling against his workers, Abe accepts their proposal to become owners of the firm along with himself so that all are responsible and get their share of the profits. Having learnt this new way, which is one kind of socialist enterprise, Abe abandons the old ideals of individual ownership and power and decides to give himself and his wife Esther more time to enjoy the basic pleasures of existence. He tells her: 'The grass still grows, and the trees are still here, and there's still enough sun for us to took at!' He now speaks of a bright future for himself and Esther: 'There's new ways to live ... young ways, and we gotta learn them.'[10] The new ways represent the future, the coming socialist society.

In the next version, *No Villain*, the radical message has been sharpened. The unjust concentration of economic power is seen as the main flaw of capitalism. Socialism is the answer, and Ben Simon, the Marxist, explains the basics of 'communism,' as it is now called, to his mother. It means the transfer of ownership of the means of production to the workers, who then will control their economic situation.[11]

Esther worries about her family and does not understand what is happening in society. She laments: 'My God, my good God, what makes us move like this? Where we don't want to go?.'[12] Her cry is that of the unenlightened multitudes who cannot see beyond appearances. But Ben knows that it is the economic system that is responsible. His brother Arnold, also a Marxist, condemns strikebreaking, knowing that the strike weapon is vital for workers. There are certain principles one has to stand up for if one wants to be a socialist. Loyalty to the common man, to the ideals of solidarity and a better society, is more important than loyalty to family. The conflict between these two later became very prominent in *All My Sons*.

At the end of the play Ben has had enough, both of capitalism, egoistic individualism and old-fashioned, clannish ways. Religion, in this case Judaism, diverts people's attention from the causes of the problem and, like the economic system, it too must go. Scientific reason, as proclaimed by Marx, must replace old superstitions. Ben's grandfather has died, but the young man throws out the pious Jews who pray by the old man's coffin. He also tells Mr. Roth, Helen's wealthy father, to depart. It is time, Ben declares, to start on a new path and clear the way for the socialist future: 'For us it begins, Arny and I ... for us there begins ... sort of a fight ... so that you'll know that this ... will never be in our lives ... I've got to build something bigger ... Something that'll change this deeply ... to the bottom ... it's the only way dad.'[13] Later, in *Death of a Salesman*, there was to be another funeral scene where the son, now called Biff, also refuses to carry on in the manner of his father, for whom business success overrides everything else.

The last version of this play is from 1939 and is entitled *The Grass Still Grows: A Comedy*. Arnold Simon is now a doctor, and Sam Roth and Helen figure more prominently than before. Roth's unscrupulous fights against trade unions have ensured his wealth, and Abe and Esther, as before, are looking to a marriage between Ben and Helen as the solution to the financial problems of the family. Roth, a hardboiled tycoon, can be seen as an early version of Willy Loman's elder brother, the deceased Ben, an archetypal figure of the American captain of industry. This is a man without a conscience, as Miller sees it, the product of the inhuman socio-economic conditions established by capitalism.

Ben Simon loves Louise, his father's bookkeeper, but he may have to marry Helen. Arnold warns him: 'If you break this up, neither of you will ever get an equal value in return.'[14] Arnold himself has begun to regret his decision to become a doctor, perceiving that he has been inordinately driven by careerism. He eventually marries Helen so that Ben is free to marry Louise. As before, Abe decides to go into partnership with his workers. He now supports Ben's choice with regard to marriage and declares: 'I'm proud, because for one of the few times in my life, I saw a man obey himself.'[15] This is also what Biff Loman finally does, though in his case there is no support to be had from the father.

In the published plays, Miller departs from the agitprop style he used during the thirties and conveys his criticism and his socialist ideas in a more oblique manner. *The Man Who Had All the Luck*, the first of these works, takes place in a small town and its hero, David Frieber, is involved in businesses such as automobile repair and mink farming. However, the evils of competitive, anarchic capitalism are still the main theme. David is in love with and wants to marry Hester Falk, whose father, significantly, is rich. David is only a car mechanic, but things change when Gustav Eberson, another mechanic, helps him fix the car of a man called Dan Dibble. David takes the credit for the difficult repair job, which was really Eberson's doing, and thus gains a new stature in the community and gets his big opportunity in business. The theme of business crookedness is thus introduced at the start of the play. In the economic jungle of capitalist society there are no rules except one, to survive and win, and even mendacity is more or less permissible if it leads to financial success.

David then marries Hester, whose father dies, and enjoys his new-found wealth. But he has forgotten one thing, his conscience, and his guilt lies heavily upon him, threatening his sanity. When a son is born to him, he starts to believe that he is losing money, and this becomes a delusion. Having taken up mink farming, he also becomes obsessed with the minks and their well-being. Hester explains that David has been certain that his child would die. On account of guilt, he cannot believe that he will actually have everything he wants.

At the end of the play it is revealed to David that he unwittingly has given his minks contaminated feed and that they will die unless the feed is removed. But Hester tells him to stay in the house and let the minks die. She knows that it is only by atoning for his initial fraud in some way that her husband can regain his self-respect: "Whatever it is that hangs over your head, take it in your hands and kill it now! ... Davey, you're a good man, good with your hands, you've always been a good man. Understand it!"[16] He finally realizes this himself, letting the minks die and deciding to share his business with Gustav Eberson. The killing of the minks is rather odd in itself, but it makes sense as David's exoneration of the guilt instilled in him by his unconscionable pursuit of capitalist ends.

In *All My Sons*, Miller's first successful drama, the attack on the anti-social consequences of capitalism is more forcefully expressed than in *The Man Who Had All the Luck*. Joe Keller, a wartime manufacturer of airplane engines, ships out a number of faulty cylinder heads in order to keep his defense contract and stay in business. This leads to the death of twenty-one fighter pilots. Keller is arrested, but succeeds in laying the blame on his partner, Steve Deever, and goes scot free.

Miller wants to show that Keller's crimes derive from the amoral nature of capitalist competition.[17] This man has acted according to the laws of the competitive economic environment that he is familiar with and is largely unaware, during the major part of the play, of how his conscience has been corrupted. His guilt, however, like that of David Frieber, will not let him alone and emerges, half consciously, in various ways. For example, he reveals it by telling Deever's daughter Ann that he is ready to give her father a job once he gets out of prison. Ann is engaged to Joe's son Larry. Keller is also worried to learn that George, Ann's brother, is coming to visit and fears, with good reason, that his crimes will be exposed by this man. It is also suggested that Kate, Keller's wife, knows the truth about her husband and is ready to collaborate with him in a cover-up. She warns him against George and tells him to be smart and protect them all. She is an accessory to his misdeeds, and their other son, Chris, eventually accuses both of his parents of moral failure.

In the last part of the play, Keller's secret is finally brought to light, and he has to confess to Chris that he was the one who told Deever to ship out the faulty engine parts. In keeping with Miller's effort to present Keller as a victim of capitalist conditions, he regards himself as one who was forced to do what he did. He knows too well that there is no mercy in the market-place and that ruin means disaster, pure and simple. Because he has been compelled to fight all his life for a place in the sun, economically speaking, he has lost his moral bearings and can think only of himself. Capitalism, the free play of economic forces, is responsible for Keller's extreme individualism and abdication of all responsibility for anyone but himself and his family.

Against these callous attitudes Miller marshals his attack, showing us that murder and betrayal of the worst sort can result from them. Using Chris Keller as his mouthpiece, but without presenting him as a Marxist, he voices his criticism of the existing capitalist order and hints at a socialist alternative, a world based on collective ownership and the brotherhood of man. Chris had found such a community when at the front, among soldiers whose extreme situation had taught them the true values of love and fellowship. The revelation of his father's crimes sharpens Chris's insight into the amorality of the capitalist 'rat race,' as he calls it.[18] Shocked and furious, he castigates his father for the criminal narrowness of his perceptions: 'Is that as far as you can see, the business? What is that, the world—the business? What the hell do you mean, you did it for me? Don't you have a country? Don't you live in the world? What the hell are you?' (116). This rejection of *laissez-faire* individualism and its fixation on economic achievement to the exclusion of all else is the same as that expressed by Ben Simon in *No Villain*.

Keller, however, true to his outlook and experience, insists that his committing them for the family has got to excuse his offences and that he had to act as he did: 'Who worked for nothin' in that war? When they work for nothin,' I'll work for nothin.' Did they ship a gun or a truck outa Detroit before they got their price? Is that clean? It's dollars and cents, nickels and dimes, what's clean? Half the Goddam country is got to go if I go?' (125). But when he learns that Larry has committed suicide out of grief and shame over his father's conduct, Keller has to face the fact that his actions have had terrible consequences. He can no longer disregard his guilt and is so overwhelmed by remorse that he shoots himself. Both the death of the innocent fliers and the suicide of Keller and Larry are portrayed as direct results of a capitalist economy merciless enough to drive a man like Keller to his abominable acts.[19]

Miller's emphasis on a socialist, collectivist morality also emerges in Chris's final chastisement of a parental generation corrupted by mindless economic egoism: 'You can be better! Once and for all you can know there's a universe of people outside and you're responsible to it' (126). Keller's death is also a step in this direction, showing his recognition of guilt and thus of a wider responsibility. Notions of a socialist future are also suggested in what Kate Keller says at the end. She admonishes Chris to put the past behind him and start to live life to the full; for him a new society may come into being where the values of life and love will assume their rightful place. Thus the sentiments of Abe and Esther Simon in *The Grass Still Grows*, the rejection of capitalist materialism and the love of life, reemerge in the new context of *All My Sons*.

Death of a Salesman is perhaps even more effective in its anti-capitalist thrust than *All My Sons*, and it, too, is rooted in the playwright's early, agonized reactions to the Depression. Marxism had taught him that this disaster was one of the vagaries of capitalism, and his early, militant stance is suggested in an observation recorded in a notebook containing an early version of the play: 'The restrictions, like all tyrannies, exist by default of revolutionary resistance.'[20] The reference is to formal conventions in drama, but the choice of words reveals a political radicalism also.

As in the other plays, victimization by the free play of economic forces is the main theme of *Death of a Salesman*. It is suggested in the initial stage direction: 'A melody is heard, played upon a flute. It is small and fine, telling of grass and trees and the horizon. Before us is the salesman's house. We are aware of towering, angular shapes behind it, surrounding it on all sides' (130). The people in the house are threatened and overwhelmed by the tall buildings, symbols of the crushing power of those who win out in a capitalist struggle that has no room for failures and losers.

Willy Loman, the ageing salesman, is worn out to the point of breakdown by his many years on the road. But he remains a firm believer in capitalist values and has transferred his hope of success to his son Biff. Willy is a dreamer, and the play contrasts his dreams with the harsh realities of failure and mediocrity that he tries to shut out of his mind. Corrupted, or brainwashed by the system, Willy is blind to its destructiveness and is obsessed by his plans for Biff.

Biff, however, has begun to rebel against his father's ideas and to feel his way towards different standards, meaning those that Miller associates with the socialist society. Unlike his brother Happy, he has 'allowed himself to turn his face toward defeat,' (136) and even this becomes a possible source of strength for him. His lack of conventional success is slowly teaching him, not that he is worthless, but that he may not be cut out for a business career and may actually be better off without it. He is trying to understand himself and discover his real identity, this also being an aim of socialism as Miller understood it. But Biff is not yet sure of himself, in the first part of the play, and still feels guilty for not being a success. He has returned to his parents in a last attempt to fulfill his father's dreams.

Happy, who has a good job and wants to get further ahead, also has doubts about his own careerism but cannot find anything to put in its place. Biff struggles with this issue, searching for and finally finding another path for himself. However, his father remains a man whose self-respect depends entirely on his role as a breadwinner and useful cog in the production machine. He worships the memory of Ben, the youth who walked into the jungle of Africa at the age of seventeen and came out rich at twenty-one, a powerful *entrepreneur*. What Willy fails to realize is that only a very few can hope to be that successful. His greatest illusion is his belief in the capitalist myth that every man can succeed in business if he only uses his opportunities. Willy is also haunted by the equally superhuman success ideal embodied in his grandfather, a heroic pioneer figure who drove across America with his family, supporting them all by selling flutes that he made himself.

The scene in which Willy is fired by his young boss Howard is a perfect illustration of the logic of the capitalist economic mechanism. Willy has been with the firm since before Howard was born, but the almost familial relationship between these two still counts for nothing. Mortally afraid of ruin, like Keller, Willy appeals to Howard's conscience, reminding him how long and faithfully he has worked for the company, but to no avail. Howard is not evil, however; he is even able to sympathize with Willy's plight, but this in no way interferes with his decision to fire an ageing employee who can no longer ring up any sales. Howard, like Ben or Charley, a businessman who is Willy's friend and neighbor, abides by the law of profitability first that is supreme in the world of capitalist business. He is impersonal about it, again like Charley or Ben, regarding it as a law of nature.[21]

Wanting to help Willy, Charley offers him a job, but the former refuses to take it, feeling that it would be a kind of charity and would violate the image he has of himself as a self-reliant, honorable individual who does not depend on others. Rugged individualism is the ideology of the *laissez-faire* capitalism that he believes in so deeply. But the facts are that Willy's failure is destroying him and that Biff's similar fate makes his father reject him. The all-important success ideal prevents Willy from perceiving Biff as a person and an individual. Capitalist values distort and destroy what should have been a rewarding human relationship between father and son.

The horrifying consequences of a blind adherence to these values emerge in Willy's decision to commit suicide so that his life insurance payment will enable Biff to rise in the world. But Biff, like Chris Keller, instead becomes the vehicle through which Miller subtly introduces his alternative socialist perceptions and values into his work. Biff thus becomes the only character in the drama who really understands the destructive nature of capitalist priorities and feels pity and concern for his father, exclaiming: 'I can't bear to look at his face!' (115). He tries to make Willy understand the realities of their situation, which is that their lives have been dominated by a dream that is no better than a lie. Biff has realized that the whole family are victims, in various ways and like most people, of capitalist oppression and false standards. They are basically downtrodden people, 'a dime a dozen' (132). But this, of course, is the very thing that Willy refuses to admit, and he denies it furiously. Biff tries to impress upon him that they ought to lower their expectations and rely on the comforts of love and human caring. Willy, however, is not willing to correct his capitalist hierarchy of values and accuses Biff of betrayal. His son, he says, is 'vengeful' and 'spiteful' (132). But Biff continues his attempt to break through to his father's feelings and establish a genuine connection and respect between them. Hence his plaintive cry: 'Pop, I'm nothing ... I'm just what I am, that's all' (133).

In this central scene, Willy does perceive that his son wants to show him his love, but is unable to respond to this in a simple way. Instead, and in keeping with his blinkered vision, he grotesquely interprets Biff's love as yet another sign of his potentially glorious future, or as a part of the fine personality that will help making him rich: 'That boy—that boy is going to be magnificent!' (133). The insurance money will yet secure Biff's success, he thinks, and is deluded enough to assume that his son will be thankful for the sacrifice he is making,

But at Willy Loman's grave it is capitalism and the dreams it is responsible for that are indicted. Looking back on his father's life, Biff firmly declares: 'He had the wrong dreams. All, all wrong' (138). *Death of a Salesman* suggests that the right dreams are opposed to rapacious capitalism and that they are about justice, love and genuine selfhood as envisaged by Marxism.

During the first twenty years of his work as a playwright, then, a radical political message is present in Miller's plays, published and unpublished. The author's main concern is with the destructive effects of an unfettered capitalist economy. His focus is always on the human victims of the system, and he shows how the victimization has its fundamental causes in capitalism's exclusive and callous pursuit of maximum profits. In *Honors at Dawn*, workers are exploited and underpaid, in *The Great Disobedience* the prison is full of people who have been driven to crime because of unemployment and destitution. In the various versions of *No Villain* Abe Simon faces loss of livelihood because of the ruthless practices of big companies, both against people like himself and workers. Abe is also harmed in another way by the desperate situation in which he finds himself. He begins to bargain with his conscience, wanting his son to marry a rich girl for the sake of her money.

In the printed plays, this impairment of a person's conscience and sanity as a consequence of intolerable economic pressures is the main concern of Miller the anti-capitalist. David Frieber cheats his way to success, encouraged by lawless capitalism. Similarly, Joe Keller is driven to lawbreaking to avoid economic disaster, his actions parallel to those of the men who end up in prison in *The Great Disobedience*. In *Death of a Salesman* the jobless Willy Loman has become mentally disturbed, his suicide for the sake of money an eloquent testimony to the corrosive effects of the tyrannical success ideal extolled by his society. Willy is a victim, both directly and indirectly, of the logic of a capitalism which says that human worth is proportional to economic achievement. Taken as a whole, these dramas build a powerful indictment against the American capitalist system that Miller knew, but they do not stop at that point. Whether openly or more discreetly, they suggest the possibility of another, just and humane society. This new, socialist world will be built on the principles of love, mutual concern and sharing rather than competition.

NOTES

1. Miller has described his own and his friends' early adoption of Marxism in his autobiography: 'We enjoyed a certain unity within ourselves by virtue of a higher consciousness bestowed by our expectation of a socialist evolution of the planet.' *Timebends: A Life* (New York, 1987), p. 70.

2. In the early forties Miller attended a Marxist study group and was proposed for membership in the American Communist Party. In *The New York Times*, May 25, 1947, his name appeared on a list of sponsors of the World Youth Festival, organized by the communist World Federation of Democratic Youth. See J. Schlueter and J. K. Flanagan, *Arthur Miller* (New York, 1987), pp. 6, 146.

3. Interpreting Marx, R. W. Miller states that: 'under socialism and communism, most people are less dominated, more in possession of their lives, since they are better able to develop their capacities in light of their own assessments of their needs. Moreover, their interactions will be governed to a greater extent than now by mutual well-wishing and concern.' 'Marx and Morality,' in *Marxism*, ed. J. R. Pennock and J. W. Chapman (New York, 1983), p. 60.

4. *Honors at Dawn*, typescript, undated, in the Harlan Hatcher Graduate Library, University of Michigan, Ann Arbor, p. 28.

5. *Honors at Dawn* has been criticized for its political content: 'The broader struggle in *Honors at Dawn* is clearly the Marxist battle between the ogre of capitalism and the emerging proletariat [sic] hero. It is a duel rigidly fixed in the leftist cast of its times, and its resolution is as predictable as a *Daily Worker* editorial on H. L. Hunt.' Benjamin Nelson, *Arthur Miller: Portrait of a Playwright* (London, 1970), p. 26. But this is to ignore the full force of the economic emergency of the Depression. Capitalism was indeed an ogre then, and socialism seemed to offer a solution.

6. *The Great Disobedience*, typescript, undated, in the Harlan Hatcher Graduate Library, p. 11.

7. *Ibid.*, p, 30.

8. *The Grass Still Grows*, typescript, undated, in the Harlan Hatcher Graduate Library, p. 42.

9. *The Grass Still Grows*, typescript, undated, in the Harry Ransom Humanities Research Center, University of Texas, Austin, p. i.

10. *Ibid.*, p. 44.

11. This manuscript also includes an epigraph from Engels, attacking what is regarded as a parasitic capitalist class 'which, without in any way participating in production, won for itself the directing role over production as a whole and threw the producers into economic subjection.' *No Villain*, typescript, dated 1939, in the Harry Ransom Humanities Research Center, p. i.

12. *Ibid.*, p. 38.

13. *Ibid.*, p. 60.

14. *The Grass Still Grows: A Comedy*, typescript, dated 1939, in the Harry Ransom Humanities Research Center, p. 13.

15. *Ibid.*, p. 21.

16. *Cross-Section: A Collection of New American Writing*, ed. E. Seaver (New York, 1944), p. 550.

17. In this case, Miller's intentions have been made clear by himself: 'I was trying to be a Marxist, and "All My Sons" could not have been written in the precise way it was by someone who was not trying to be a Marxist.' 'Introduction,' *Collected Plays*, typescript, undated, in the Harry Ransom Humanities Research Center, p. 2.

18. *Plays: One* (London, 1958), p. 80. Quotations from *All My Sons* and *Death of a Salesman* are from this edition and are given page references in brackets.

19. Steven R. Centola blames Keller for acting in 'bad faith' because he thinks he has only two choices, to save his business or 'watch his family starve.' 'Bad Faith and *All My Sons*,' in *Arthur Miller's All My Sons*, ed. H. Bloom (New York, 1988), p. 128. But the point is exactly that Keller feels, wrongly or rightly, that these are his only choices, given the society he lives in.

20. Notebook, in longhand, undated, in the Harry Ransom Humanities Research Center.

21. Brian Parker argues that because Howard and Charley, both capitalists, are ordinary men and not evil, *Death of a Salesman* cannot be an anti-capitalist play. But the fact that these are not bad men does not change the workings of the system that they represent. See 'Point of View in Arthur Miller's *Death of a Salesman*,' *Arthur Miller: A Collection of Critical Essays* (Englewood Cliffs, 1969), p. 99.

Chronology

1915   Born Arthur Asher Miller on October 17 in New York City to Isadore and Augusta ("Gussie") Miller.

1920–28   Attends Public School No. 24 in Harlem.

1923   Sees his first play at the Schubert Theatre.

1928   Has bar mitzvah ceremony at Avenue M Temple.

1929   Isadore's business goes bankrupt because of the Depression.

1933   Graduates from Abraham Lincoln High School. Registers for night school at City College but quits after two weeks.

1934   Enters the University of Michigan, Ann Arbor, majoring in journalism.

1936   Writes the play *No Villain* in only six days and receives the Avery Hopwood Award.

1940   Marries Mary Grace Slattery.

1944   Daughter Jane is born on September 7. *The Man Who Had All the Luck* is published and wins Theatre Guild National Prize.

1945   Publishes his first novel, entitled *Focus*.

1947   Son Robert is born on May 31. *All My Sons* opens on Broadway and receives The New York Drama Critics' Circle Award.

1949   *Death of a Salesman* opens in Philadelphia, then New York; wins the Pulitzer Prize and several additional awards.

1950	Meets Marilyn Monroe in Hollywood.
1953	*The Crucible* opens on Broadway.
1956	Divorces Mary Grace Slattery in June and marries Marilyn Monroe.
1957	Rewrites the short story "The Misfits" into a screenplay for his wife Marilyn to star in. Convicted of contempt of Congress for not naming suspected Communists.
1958	Contempt conviction overturned.
1961	*The Misfits* opens in movie theaters, and Marilyn files for divorce.
1962	Marries Ingeborg (Inge) Morath. Later in the year, Marilyn Monroe dies of a drug overdose.
1963	Daughter Rebecca Augusta is born in September; Miller publishes a children's book called *Jane's Blanket*.
1964	Elected president of International PEN (Poets, Essayists, and Novelists).
1968	The one millionth copy of *Death of a Salesman* is sold.
1970	Miller's works are banned in the Soviet Union as a result of his work to free politically resistant writers.
1978	*The Theater Essays of Arthur Miller* is published. Miller attends the 25th anniversary of *The Crucible* in Belgium.
1981	The second volume of *Arthur Miller's Collected Plays* is published.
1983	Directs *Death of a Salesman* in China with a Chinese cast.
1984	*Death of a Salesman* is revived on Broadway with Dustin Hoffman starring as Willy Loman.
1987	Writes his autobiography, *Timebends: A Life*.
1997	*The Crucible* is made into a feature film starring Winona Rider and Daniel Day-Lewis.
1998	Receives the Senator Claiborne Pell Award for lifetime achievement in the arts.
1999	*Death of a Salesman* is revived on Broadway for its 50th anniversary. Miller is awarded the coveted Dorothy and Lillian Gish Prize.

2000	Miller's collected essays from 1944 to 2000, *Echoes Down the Corridor*, are published.
2001	*Untitled*, a previously unpublished one-act play written for Vaclav Havel, appears in New York. Miller is awarded an NEH Fellowship
2002	New York City revivals of *The Man Who Had All the Luck* and *The Crucible*. Inge Morath dies.

Works by Arthur Miller

The Man Who Had All the Luck, A Collection of New American Writing,
    1944
Situation Normal, 1944
Focus, 1945
All My Sons, 1947
Death of a Salesman, 1949
An Enemy of the People, adaptation, 1950
The Crucible, 1953
A View from the Bridge, 1955
A Memory of Two Mondays, 1955
Arthur Miller's Collected Plays, 1957
The Misfits, 1961
After the Fall, 1964
Incident at Vichy, 1964
I Don't Need You Any More, 1967
The Price, 1968
In Russia (with Inge Morath), 1969
The Portable Arthur Miller, Harold Clurman (ed), 1971
The Creation of the World and Other Business, 1973
In the Country (with Inge Morath), 1977
The Theater Essays of Arthur Miller, Robert A. Martin (ed), 1978
Chinese Encounters (with Inge Morath), 1979

Playing for Time, 1980

After the Fall: A Play in Two Acts, 1985

Danger: Memory!: Two Plays: I Can't Remember Anything and Clara, 1987

The Archbishop's Ceiling/The American Clock: Two Plays, 1989

Everybody Wins: A Screenplay, 1990

The Ride Down Mount Morgan, 1991

Broken Glass, 1995

Homely Girl, A Life and Other Stories, 1997

Mr. Peters' Connection, 1999

Echoes Down the Corridor: Collected Essays, 1947–1999, 2000

Works about Arthur Miller

Bigsby, C.W.E. "What Price Arthur Miller? An Analysis of *The Price*." *Twentieth Century Literature: A Scholarly and Critical Journal*, Vol. 16 (1970): 16–25.

———. "The Fall and After: Arthur Miller's Confession." *Modern Drama*, Vol.10 (1967): 124–136.

Bliquez, Guerin. "Linda's Role in *Death of a Salesman*." *Modern Drama*, Vol. 10 (1968): 383–386.

Bonnet, Jean-Marie. "Society vs. the Individual in Arthur Miller's *The Crucible*." *English Studies: A Journal of English Language and Literature*, Vol. 63, No. 1 (February 1982): 32–36.

Bronson, David. "*An Enemy of the People*: A Key to Arthur Miller's Art and Ethics." *Comparative Drama*, Vol. 2 (1968–1969): 229–247.

Brucher, Richard T. "Willy Loman and The Soul of a New Machine: Technology and the Common Man." *Journal of American Studies*, Vol. 17, No. 3 (December 1983): 325–336.

Calarco, N. Joseph. "Production As Criticism: Miller's *The Crucible*." *Educational Theater Journal*, Vol. 29 (1977): 354–361.

Centola, Steven R. "Family Values in *Death of a Salesman*." *CLA Journal: A Quarterly Official Publication of The College Language Association*, Vol. XXXVII, No. 1 (September 1993): 19–41.

Clurman, Harold. "Director's Notes: *Incident at Vichy*." *The Drama Review*, Vol. 9, No. 4 (1965): 77–90.

Corrigan, Robert W. "The Achievement of Arthur Miller." *Comparative Drama*, Vol. 12 (1968): 141–160.

Curtis, Penelope. "*The Crucible*." *The Critical Review*, Vol. 8 (1965) 45–58.

Davison, Richard Allan. "Arthur Miller and Other Critics of the Fifth Column." *North Dakota Quarterly*, Vol. 65, No. 3 (1998): 26–34.

Decter, Midge. "The Witches of Arthur Miller." *Commentary*, Vol. 103, No. 3 (March 1997): 54–56.

Ditsky, John. "Stone, Fire and Light: Approaches to *The Crucible*." *North Dakota Quarterly*, Vol. 46, No. 2 (1978): 65–72.

Fender, Stephen. "Precision and Pseudo Precision in *The Crucible*." *Journal of American Studies*, Vol. 1 (1967): 87–98.

Ferguson, Alfred R. "The Tragedy of the American Dream in *Death of a Salesman*." *Thought: A Review of Culture and Ideal*, Vol. 53 (1978): 83–98.

Field, B.S., Jr. *Twentieth Century Literature: A Scholarly and Critical Journal*. Vol. 18 (1972): 19–24.

Gross, Barry Edward. "Peddler and Pioneer in *Death of a Salesman*." *Modern Drama*, Vol. 7 (1965): 405–410.

Hadomi, Leah. "Dramatic Rhythm in *Death of a Salesman*." *Modern Drama*, Vol. XXXI, No. 2 (June 1988): 157–174.

Hagopian, John V. "Arthur Miller: The Salesman's Two Cases." *Modern Drama*, Vol. 6 (1963): 117–125.

Hatman, Ronald. "Arthur Miller: Between Satire and Society." Encounter, Vol. 37, 73–79.

Hendrickson, Gary P. "The Last Analogy: Arthur Miller's Witches and America's Domestic Communists." *The Midwest Quarterly*, Vol. 33 (Summer 1992): 447–455.

Henian, Yuan. "*Death of A Salesman* in Beijing." Chinese Literature, No. 10 (1983): 103–109.

Hill, Philip G. "The Crucible: A Structural View." *Modern Drama*, Vol. 10 (1967): 312–317.

Hurd, Myles R. "Angels and Anxieties in Miller's *A View from the Bridge*." *Notes on Contemporary Literature*, Vol. 13, No. 4 (September 1983): 4–6.

Jackson, Esther Merle. "*Death of A Salesman*: Tragic Myth in the Modern Theatre." *College Language Association Journal*, Vol. 7 (1963): 63–76.

Jacobson, Irving. "Family Dreams in *Death of A Salesman*." *American Literature: A Journal of Literary History, Criticism, and Bibliography*, Vol. 47 (1975): 247–258.

King, Robert L. Review of *The Price*. *The North American Review*, Vol. 279, No. 4 (July/August 1994): 45–46.

Marino, Stephen. "Arthur Miller's 'Weight of Truth' in *The Crucible*." *Modern Drama*, Vol. XXXVIII, No. 4 (Winter 1995): 488–495.

Martin, Robert A. "Arthur Miller and the Meaning of Tragedy." *Modern Drama*, Vol. 13 (1970): 34–39.

Meyer, Jeffrey. "A Portrait of Arthur Miller." *Virginia Quarterly Review: A National Journal of Literature and Discussion*, Vol. 76, No. 3 (Summer 2000): 416–435.

Miller, Jeanne-Marie A. "Odets, Miller and Communism." *College Language Association Journal*, Vol.19 (1976): 484–493.

Moss, Leonard. "Arthur Miller and the Common Man's Language." *Modern Drama*, Vol. 7 (1964): 52–59.

Murray, Edward. "Point of View in *After the Fall*." *College Language Association Journal*, Vol. 10 (1966): 135–142

Oberg, Arthur K. "*Death of A Salesman* and Arthur Miller's Search for Style." *Criticism: A Quarterly for Literature and the Arts*, Vol. 9 (1967): 303–311.

O'Neal, Michael J. "History, Myth, and Name Magic in Arthur Miller's *The Crucible*." *CLIO: A Journal of Literature, History, and the Philosophy of History*, Vol. 12, No. 2 (Winter 1983): 111–122.

Otten, Terry. "*Death of A Salesman* at Fifty—Still 'Coming Home to Roost.'" *Texas Studies in Literature and Language*, Vol. 41, No. 3 (Fall 1999): 280–309.

Popkin, Henry. "Arthur Miller's *The Crucible*." *College English*, Vol. 26 (1964): 139–146.

Ribkoff, Fred. "Shame, Guilt, Empathy, and the Search for Identity in Arthur Miller's *Death of A Salesman*." *Modern Drama*, Vol. 43, No. 1 (Spring 2000): 48–55.

Schissel, Wendy. "Re(dis)covering the Witches in Arthur Miller's *The Crucible*: A Feminist Reading." *Modern Drama*, Vol. XXXVII, No. 3 (Fall 1994): 461–473.

Smith, Iris. "Authors in America: Tony Kushner, Arthur Miller, and Anna Deavere Smith." *The Centennial Review*, Vol. XXX, No. 1 (Winter 1996): 125–142.

Stinson, John J. "Structure in *After the Fall*: The Relevance of the Maggie Episodes to the Main Themes and the Christian Symbolism." *Modern Drama*, Vol. 10 (1967): 233–240.

Trowbridge, Clinton W. "Arthur Miller: Between Pathos and Tragedy." *Modern Drama*, Vol. 10 (1967): 221–232.

Wandor, Michelene. Review of *The Archbishop's Ceiling*. *Plays and Players*, No. 400 (January 1987): 25–26.

Wells, Arvin R. "The Living and the Dead in *All My Sons*." *Modern Drama*, Vol. 7 (1964): 46–51.

Willett, Ralph. "A Note on Arthur Miller's *The Price*." *Journal of American Studies*, Vol. 5 (1971): 307–310.

Contributors

HAROLD BLOOM is Sterling Professor of the Humanities at Yale University and Henry W. and Albert A. Berg Professor of English at the New York University Graduate School. He is the author of over 20 books, including *Shelley's Mythmaking* (1959), *The Visionary Company* (1961), *Blake's Apocalypse* (1963), *Yeats* (1970), *A Map of Misreading* (1975), *Kabbalah and Criticism* (1975), *Agon: Toward a Theory of Revisionism* (1982), *The American Religion* (1992), *The Western Canon* (1994), and *Omens of Millennium: The Gnosis of Angels, Dreams, and Resurrection* (1996). *The Anxiety of Influence* (1973) sets forth Professor Bloom's provocative theory of the literary relationships between the great writers and their predecessors. His most recent books include *Shakespeare: The Invention of the Human*, a 1998 National Book Award finalist, and *How to Read and Why*, which was published in 2000. In 1999, Professor Bloom received the prestigious American Academy of Arts and Letters Gold Medal for Criticism.

COOKIE LOMMEL started her career as a journalist in the entertainment industry, and has since interviewed hundreds of film, television, and music personalities as an on-camera reporter for CNN. She has also written biographies of Madame C. J. Walker, Robert Church, and Johnnie L. Cochran.

NEIL HEIMS is a freelance writer, editor, and researcher. He has a Ph.D. in English from the City University of New York.

ORM ÖVERLAND is a Professor of English at the University of Bergen, Norway. Among his works are *Western Home: A Literary History of Norwegian American* (1997).

MARIANNE BORUCH is a poet and a Professor of English at Purdue University, and Director of the Creative Writing Program.

HELGE NORMANN NILSEN teaches at the University of Trondheim and is the author of *Hart Crane's Divided Vision: An Analysis of "The Bridge"* (1980).

INDEX